Accelerate

A SKILLS-BASED
SHORT COURSE

INTERMEDIATE

Series editor: Philip Prowse

PATRICIA LODGE · *BETH WRIGHT-WATSON*

MACMILLAN
HEINEMANN
English Language Teaching

Macmillan Education
Between Towns Road, Oxford OX4 3PP, UK
A division of Macmillan Publishers Limited
Companies and representatives throughout the world

ISBN 0 435 28264 6

Heinemann is a registered trademark of Reed Educational and Professional Publishing Limited

First published 1995

Designed by Ken Vail Graphic Design
Cover design by Threefold Design
Cover photograph by Frank Orel/Tony Stone Images
Illustrated by: Ilsa Capper, Jo Dennis, Clive Goodyer,
Amanda Hall, Gillian Martin, Pat Murray, Jake Tebbit,
Alan Vincent, Len Jan Vis, Margaret Welbank.

Photographs by BBC Picture Library p45; Stephen
Read/Anthony Blake Picture Library p62; John
Miller/Collections p40; Dr E R Gruber/The Fortean
Picture Library p52; Sally and Richard Greenhill p10;
Greenpeace Communications p22 (2, 6); Robert Harding
Picture Library p14(a), (c), (d), (f); The Image Bank
p17(b, m); Susan de Math/*The Independent* p42; John
Voos/*The Independent* p59; Planet Earth Pictures p38;
Jennie Woodcock/Reflections p22(4), 57; Rex Features
p8(1), 22(5), 25(t), (m, l), (m, r), 26, 36, 46, 62; David
Drain/Still Pictures p60(t, b); Tony Stone Images p8(r),
16, 17 (t, l) (t, r) (t, m) (b, l), 24(b), 56, 82; Telegraph
Colour Library p17(b, r), 60(m); Zefa-Sharpshooters p51.

Commissioned photography by Paul Freestone p18,
22(3), 23, 62 and Chris Honeywell p14(b), (e), 22(l), 23,
58.

The authors would like to thank their families; Richard,
Oran, John, Kathryn and Helen.
They would also like to thank Lyn Kissenger, Louise
Brünjes, Marc Beeby and Sarah Comley for their help
with the material.

The publishers would like to thank Sarah Crake and
Ann Studholme.

Printed in Hong Kong

2004   2003   2002   2001
18 17 16 15 14 13 12 11

Contents

Map of the book

	Language focus	Skills focus
Unit 1 *Learning languages*		
Lesson 1 Helping yourself Discussing strategies for learning languages	Question formation *Yes/No* questions *Wh-* questions Subject questions	**Speaking:** fluency **Listening** for specific information
Lesson 2 Traveller's tales One person's experience of living in another country	Order of adjectives *-ing* form and infinitive	**Listening:** intensive listening **Speaking:** fluency
Lesson 3 Lots of languages The experiences of a multi-lingual family	*used to* and *would* for past habits and states	**Reading:** extensive reading **Speaking:** exchanging information
Unit 2 *Jobs*		
Lesson 1 The right job A quiz to find the right job for you	Adjective formation from nouns *-ing* form and infinitive with verbs of preference	**Listening** for main ideas **Reading** a quiz
Lesson 2 Can you judge by appearances? Women who do 'men's' jobs	Present perfect simple and present perfect continuous *for* and *since*	**Reading** for detail **Speaking:** asking questions
Lesson 3 Career counsellors A careers interview	Modal verbs of obligation and advice	**Speaking:** roleplaying an interview **Listening** for detail
Unit 3 *Describing things*		
Lesson 1 The future of fashion Discussing developments in fashion	Defining relative clauses	**Reading** for specific information; predicting **Listening** to complete a table
Lesson 2 Homes A dream house and a dream room	Open conditionals Participle adjectives	**Speaking:** an information gap activity **Listening:** labelling a diagram
Lesson 3 Advertising and selling things Describing items and advertising them	Intensifiers: *very, too, enough*	**Listening** for specific information **Writing** descriptions
Unit 4 *The games people play*		
Lesson 1 New sports Information about unusual sports	Modals of deduction	**Listening** to complete a table **Writing** an advertisement
Lesson 2 The price of fun Problems of obsession	Position of adverbs of frequency Present simple for habits and routines	**Listening** to complete a table **Reading** for specific information
Lesson 3 Make your own game Designing and playing a game	Defining and non-defining relative clauses	**Listening:** a dictation **Writing:** making a game
Unit 5 *Fear of flying*		
Lesson 1 A mystery Short story: part 1	Time linkers	**Reading:** intensive reading **Speaking:** storytelling
Lesson 2 Adventure Short story: part 2	Past simple and past continuous	**Reading** for main idea **Listening** for specific information
Lesson 3 Homecoming Short story: part 3	Reported statements Reported questions	**Speaking:** roleplaying an interview **Writing** a report

	Language focus	Skills focus
Unit 6 *Right or wrong?*		
Lesson 1 Hidden secrets Smuggling through airports	The passive	**Listening:** ordering information **Reading** to complete a text
Lesson 2 Life inside An unusual prison	First conditional Revision of *Wh-* questions	**Reading** for specific information **Speaking:** taking part in a discussion
Lesson 3 Punishment Crimes and punishments	Present perfect and past simple	**Listening:** intensive listening **Speaking:** making decisions
Unit 7 *Supertots*		
Lesson 1 In business The experiences of a young businessman	*used to* + infinitive and *be/get used to* + *-ing* form *ago* and *for*	**Reading** and **listening** to complete a table
Lesson 2 In control The aspirations of parents	Comparatives and superlatives	**Speaking:** fluency **Reading** for specific information
Lesson 3 Courting tragedy The problems of young people in sport	Linking words: conjunctions; contrast, reason and result linkers *should* and *ought to* for advice	**Listening** to complete a text **Writing** a letter giving advice
Unit 8 *Alternatives*		
Lesson 1 Alternative healing Different ways to cure bad habits and solve problems	Reported speech: reporting verbs	**Reading** a diary for detail **Speaking:** comparing and exchanging information
Lesson 2 Alternative eating Vegetarians v. meat-eaters	Past simple and past perfect	**Listening** to complete a table **Speaking:** expressing opinions
Lesson 3 Alternative thinking Healing without medicine	Adjective prefixes Articles	**Listening:** ordering information **Writing** a letter requesting information
Unit 9 *Relationships*		
Lesson 1 Could they be the same person? Relationships between twins	*both, either, neither, nor* *so did …, neither/nor did …,*	**Reading** for main idea and detail **Listening** for specific information
Lesson 2 If you could choose Would you rather be a man or a woman?	Second conditional	**Listening** for main idea and detail **Speaking:** giving personal information
Lesson 3 Trading places The experience of being someone else for the day	Conditional clauses without *if* Conditional sentences with other words: *unless, as long as*	**Listening** for detail **Speaking:** talking about an imaginary situation
Unit 10 *Greener than green*		
Lesson 1 Green is the colour Environmental problems and ways to solve them	Future with *will* and *going to*	**Reading:** using information to complete a text **Writing:** making a poster
Lesson 2 The greenest school in Britain Ways to improve the environment	Revision of passives Purpose clauses	**Reading:** finding specific information **Listening** for specific information
Lesson 3 The techno-solution Science and the environment	Future predictions and possibilities	**Reading:** note-taking **Speaking:** giving an explanation

Lesson 1 *Helping yourself*

Language focus: Question formation

Skills focus: Speaking: fluency
Listening for specific information

1

Play this game in groups of four. You will need a dice and counters. The first person to finish is the winner!

START HERE

1 How long have you been learning English? Where? How?

2 Go forward 3 spaces

3 Which English pop singers do you like?

4 Do you like learning English? Why? Why not?

5 Talk about yourself for one minute.

6 How do you like travelling?
a by plane
b by car
c by coach
Why?

19 Count from 990 to 1030

20 'It's my teacher's fault when I don't learn.' Do you agree with this? Why? Why not?

21 Who is the best British sports personality in your opinion? What sport do they play?

22 Do you listen to the BBC World Service on the radio? Tell us about it.

23 Sorry! Go back 6 places

24 How do you say...?
a photograph
b photographer
c photographic
What's the difference?

7 You're going too fast! Go back 2 spaces

18 How many times have you been to England? What did you see?

31 You're too near the end! Go back 2 spaces

32 How many languages do you speak? How did you learn them?

33 Do you like working in groups or on your own? Why?

Finished! You are the WINNER

25 Are there any words in your language which are the same in English? (eg television)

8 Tell us one thing you hate doing, or you dislike other people doing.

17 Who's been studying English the longest in your group?

30 Which do you prefer and why?
a a monolingual dictionary
b a bilingual dictionary

29 Have you seen a film in English? Talk about it.

28 Find the meaning of **assimilate** as quickly as possible.

27 Which country would you like to visit most? What language do people speak there?

26 How often did you speak English last week – outside class!

9 How do you try to remember new English words?

16 Do you like reading in English? Why? Why not? Tell us about an English book you have read.

15 Say three adjectives that describe your personality.

14 ZZZzzzzz You're sleepy! Miss a turn!

13 Describe someone in the class (the others must guess who it is).

12 Say the alphabet a, b, c . . .

11 Tell everyone why you want to learn English.

10 How many English or American TV programmes do you watch in your country?

2

This is what some students do to help themselves to learn English.

> I like listening to songs and reading the words at the same time.

Abdullah

> I watch English films sometimes.

Reza

> Going to class and working is enough for me!

Premi

> I make lists of vocabulary to learn each day and pin them up on my wall.

Osmantan

Do you do any of these things? Tell the other students in your group.

3

Make a list of at least seven things you could do to learn English when you are not in class. Think about what you need and where you can go. Use your answers to numbers 9, 10, 16, 26, 30 and 32 in the game to help you.

Discuss your ideas with other groups.

4

Listen to four students talking about how they learn English outside class. Look at your group's list of ideas, and tick (✓) any of your ideas that they mention.

Write a short letter to your teacher telling him/her what you have decided to do, and why.

5

This is a word map. It shows ways of learning English outside class. Try to complete the map using ideas from the four students on the tape. There are ten gaps.

Listen again to check your answers.

6

Choose three things on the map that you would like to do to help yourself improve your English outside class time.

Are any of the ideas new to you?

Language Summary

Question formation

Yes/No questions
  Have you seen a film in English?

Wh- questions
  Which English pop singers do you like?

Subject questions
  Who's been studying English the longest in your group?

see practice page 66

Lesson 2 *Traveller's tales*

Language focus: Order of adjectives

Skills focus:　Listening: intensive listening
　　　　　　　　Speaking: fluency

1

Work in groups. Have you ever visited another country? Tell your group where you went and why you went there. Did you have any problems with the language?

2

In your groups, write a list of ten important words and phrases you need to know when you visit a country for the first time.

Example

> 1 How much does it cost?
> 2 Numbers from 1–10
> 3 Where is...?
> 4 Foods

Discuss your list with another group. Use the best ideas to make a new list of ten. You will need this list for Activity 4.

Choose the most useful word or phrase from the new list.

3

Look at the photos of Indonesia below. Do you know anything about Indonesia? How big is the country? What is the weather like there? What food do people eat there? Discuss these questions in groups.

4

Listen to Beth talking about her first visit to Indonesia. Are the words and phrases she needed the same as the list you made in Activity 2? Tick any of your words or phrases that she mentions.

5

Listen again and answer these questions.

1 What happened at the airport?
2 Which words did she need there? Write the <u>exact</u> words.
3 What happened on the journey in the car?
4 Why did she learn the words quickly?

Listen to Beth saying which words she remembered and fill in the gaps in this dictation.

I think out of all the words I learnt _____ travelling to

Indonesia, _____ _____ were the most _____ because

I _____ them all the time right from the first day. But

the words I remembered _____ were how to describe

things, my _____ in particular, and how to talk about

_____ . I think it's when you're forced to _____ new

words that you really _____ them.

6

How do you remember words?

People remember words in different ways. Look at this list and tick the methods you use.

☐ Forcing myself to use at least one new word every day.

☐ Repeating new words.

☐ Translating them and writing a list.

☐ Grouping new words – eg *houses*, *food*, etc.

☐ Writing a word with its definition.

☐ Keeping index cards.

☐ Writing the words in sentences.

☐ Sticking word cards on the bedroom wall.

☐ Spending a few minutes every day reading a list of new words.

Can you add any more ideas to this list?

Compare your answers with another student. Do you do the same things?

7

You can use word maps like the one in Lesson 1 to help you remember new vocabulary. Look at the word map below about air travel and use the words in the box to complete it.

aeroplane   airport   captain   check-in

customs   departure lounge   duty free

flight attendant   hand luggage   holdall

in-flight film   lost property   luggage

rucksack   tickets

8

Traveller's Tips, by Intertravel, is a leaflet which gives advice to people travelling abroad. Work in pairs. Write a list of six tips for people travelling anywhere in the world.

Traveller's Tips

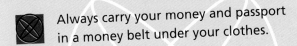
Always carry your money and passport in a money belt under your clothes.

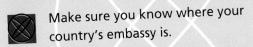
Make sure you know where your country's embassy is.

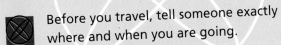
Before you travel, tell someone exactly where and when you are going.

Which are the ten best tips in the class?

Homework

Choose a topic – eg *clothes, crime,* and make your own word map. Use as many words as you can, and draw pictures to help you remember!

Language Summary

Order of adjectives
  It was a **large, square, blue, nylon** suitcase.

-ing form and infinitive:
  I **managed to remember** the vocabulary for cars.
  We **practised repeating** new words.

see practice page 67

Lesson 3 *Lots of languages*

Language focus: *used to* and *would* for past habits and states

Skills focus: Reading: extensive reading
                    Speaking: exchanging information

1

Answer the following questions on your own.

1 If you went to live in a foreign country, would you:
   a learn the language?
   b teach your children both your own language and the language of the new country?
   c celebrate your old customs?
   d adopt the customs of the new country?
   e change your religion to that of the new country?
   f let your children feel they belong to the new country?

2 If someone came to live in your country, would you expect them to do these things?

Compare your answers with other students. Do you all agree? Do you know anyone in either of these situations?

2

Look at the photo of Marie and her daughters, Adele and Klara. Listen to Marie and complete the chart below.

Name	Marie Young
Age now	
Place of birth	
Nationality	
Husband's nationality	
Number of children	
Children's ages now	
Present home	

3

Marie and Klara were interviewed about learning languages. Work in pairs. Student A – read the interview with Marie. Student B – read the interview with Klara. As you read, put the headings above the paragraphs.

MARIE

*Why two languages?   Advice from Marie   Marie's decision
Marie's method   Speaking English in France   The result*

1 Why two languages?

Because I had so many problems learning languages, and because I wanted my children to be able to talk to my Czech family, I started to speak Czech to Adele as soon as she was born. There were no problems because, as she was born in England with an English father, both the children would have spoken English sooner or later. Everything was fine until my husband came home one day and said 'Why don't we go to France?'

2 _____

At two years old Adele was quite fluent in Czech; she was advanced for her age. However, she only understood English but couldn't speak it. Like all French children, Klara and Adele would go to Maternelle (nursery school) at the age of three, so I knew they would pick up French. That's when I decided on my individual way of dealing with the problem.

3 _____

I'd say a short sentence in English first, for example 'Come here' or 'Let's go out', and I immediately repeated it in Czech. This I did for a month. Then for the second month I would say it in Czech and then repeat it in English, making sure they understood that it was the same thing in both languages. By the third month Adele was bilingual. Over the years we kept up with Czech because my mother used to visit us for three months every year.

4 _____

The most important thing to remember is that children should always know when to switch languages. When a child turns to an adult they must know in which language to speak or they may become confused.

5 _____

The children picked up French from school, and we would speak English to them at home, although they would always reply in French and would speak to each other in French. They used to go to England separately when they were young teenagers. When Adele came back she would speak English at home with us and Klara thought 'I can do that, too', so they both changed to English at home.

6 _____

Sometimes it was quite difficult, for example I used to have to help them with their homework in French but we would speak about it in English. I kept it up because they didn't use to see their father very often, so they could have forgotten English if I hadn't. At times the children felt a bit like freaks and it was annoying. However, I always said 'One day you'll be grateful'. When they were about fourteen they realised how fantastic it was. All the French kids were having trouble learning English and they could actually speak it without any real effort.

KLARA

*Childhood and feeling different   Learning Spanish
Changing from one language to another   Learning Czech
Languages for money   Problems   The future*

1 *Childhood and feeling different*

As a young child I spoke mainly French, unlike my sister who spoke Czech. I didn't really speak English although I understood it. The only time I spoke it was to my grandparents but I didn't like it. My parents would insist on speaking English at home but I would refuse to copy them. We were obnoxious children and always used to reply in French because we felt different, especially when our friends came round.

2 _____

Czech, well, I suppose I learnt that when I was tiny. I would speak it when my grandmother came. It was fun. Babishka (Grandmother) used to stay for three months, and when she first arrived it was hard, but it would always come back. However, once she didn't come so I didn't speak Czech for two years and it's become more difficult as the years have gone by.

3 _____

I never felt confused though. I was quite good at switching from each language. I had three completely different worlds and they were clear in my mind. Now I sometimes have problems switching from Spanish to Czech because neither is my mother tongue.

4 _____

When I was about twelve I started to go to this International section at the Lycee. I was put into the 'A' group because I could speak English, but I had terrible trouble reading it. I used to have tantrums because it was hard. However, the school motivated me and I said 'Right, Dad, I'm going to spend two hours a week with you doing my English'.

5 _____

Also, Mummy was good because she would give us those 'Speak English' books for French kids. She used to say she would pay us one franc a page – she never did pay us, but it was motivating.

6 _____

I first started to pick up Spanish on holiday, and later at school. I was lucky because I met some Spanish kids and they would speak to me in Spanish. Because they realised I was interested in languages, little by little I progressed.

7 _____

I feel I've mastered Spanish now and would like to learn another language, probably something different like Japanese. I really admire my parents for giving us three languages and I'd do the same if I have children. I don't know how – I'd probably have to speak to Mum to find out.

4

Look again at the text you read and do the following activity for your text. Find words or expressions in the text which mean:

Marie

1 learn without effort (paragraph 2)
2 able to speak two languages fluently (paragraph 3)
3 to change from one thing to another (paragraph 4)
4 continued (paragraph 6)
5 very strange people (paragraph 6)

Klara

1 unpleasant and annoying (paragraph 1)
2 I would always remember (paragraph 2)
3 scream and shout (paragraph 4)
4 made me really want to do it (paragraph 4)
5 learn gradually (paragraph 6)

5

Read your text carefully and answer as many of these questions as you can.

1 How many languages does Marie speak?
2 What languages did Klara's sister speak when she first learnt to talk?
3 How did Marie help her daughters learn Czech and English?
4 What rule did Marie make for children who speak more than one language?
5 Why didn't the girls have the same problems with English as French school children?
6 What languages did Klara prefer speaking when she was very young? Why?
7 Why didn't Klara have any difficulty changing from one language to another?
8 How did Klara learn Spanish?
9 What does Klara want to do in future?

Work with your partner and finish answering the questions together.

6

What advice do you think Marie and Klara would give to someone who was thinking of teaching their child more than one language? Make a list.

Homework

Read the text you did not read in class and do the vocabulary activity (Activity 4).

Language Summary

used to and *would* for past habits and states
   My mother **used to** visit us for three months every year.
   My parents **would** insist on speaking English at home.

see practice page 68

Lesson 1 *The right job*

Language focus	Adjective formation from nouns *-ing* form and infinitive with verbs of preference
Skills focus:	Listening for main ideas Reading a quiz

I

Erika is a teacher. Listen to her talking about why she chose her job. As you listen, answer these questions:

1 How did she become a teacher?
2 What is important when choosing a job?
3 Why is teaching a good job for her?

I

Work in pairs. Look at the list of adjectives and check you understand them. Which adjectives did Erika use to describe a teacher? Listen to Erika again and check your answers.

*careful   dynamic   extrovert   friendly   hard-working
imaginative   lively   logical   patient   practical   responsible
smooth-talking   sympathetic   tolerant*

I

Now look at the jobs in the box. Choose the qualities from the list of adjectives which are most important for each job. Compare your list with another pair and explain how you made your choices.

**accountant   disc jockey   environmentalist
nurse   tour guide   travelling salesperson**

I

With your partner, write down three adjectives to describe yourself, and the job you would really like to do. Do you think you have the right qualities for the job?

5

Now work on your own and do the job maze below. If you answer *yes* follow the green arrow, if you answer *no* follow the red arrow. When you have found the symbol which represents you, form a group with students who have the same symbol.

START

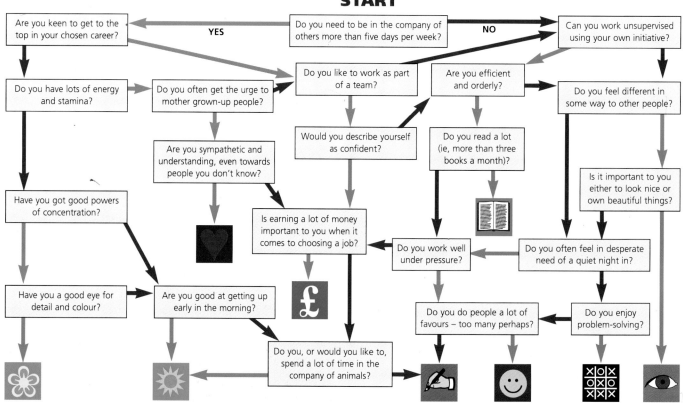

6

Find your symbol below. Choose which sentence you agree with (a, b, or c) and find out which jobs are for you.

Which of these statements most applies to you?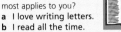
a I love writing letters.
b I read all the time.
c I read when I'm not writing.

a *You are intelligent, easy to talk to, objective, philosophical.*
The job for you: writer, TV producer, philosopher, poet.

b *You are clever, imaginative, a thinker, like to be alone.*
The job for you: lawyer, librarian, English teacher, interpreter, museum curator.

c *You are lively, thoughtful, observant, a quick-thinker, efficient.*
The job for you: journalist, editor, script writer.

Which of these statements most applies to you?
a People's problems fascinate me.
b I like helping people.
c I enjoy solving people's problems.

a *You are helpful, intelligent, tough, practical.*
The job for you: doctor, teacher, vet, nursery nurse.

b *You are calm, optimistic, friendly, hard-working, trustworthy.*
The job for you: social worker, counsellor, work with old people, nurse.

c *You are patient, wise, perceptive, expressive.*
The job for you: personnel officer, hypnotherapist, nanny, writer for magazine problem page.

Which of these statements most applies to you?
a I really love a challenging job.
b I love to see a job right through to the end result.
c I love to work with others.

a *You are clever, inquisitive, ambitious, hard-working.*
The job for you: architect, customs officer, marketing, buyer, publisher, journalist.

b *You are creative, practical, well-organised, helpful, reliable.*
The job for you: tourist officer, mechanic, chef, fashion designer, jewellery designer, publisher.

c *You are helpful, sympathetic, cautious, intelligent, good at talking to people.*
The job for you: teacher, interpreter, management consultant, personal secretary, public relations.

Which of these statements most applies to you?
a I'm extremely interested in other people.
b I'm not particularly interested in other people.
c I'm keen to improve myself and others.

a *You are artistic, sociable, self-motivated, like gossip.*
The job for you: photographer, chef, architect, journalist, musician, clothes/fashion designer.

b *You are creative, patient, a perfectionist, expressive, self-centred.*
The job for you: graphic designer, florist, model sculptor, window dresser.

c *You are creative, emotional, like people, sympathetic, big-headed, artistic.*
The job for you: model, beautician, interior designer, hairdresser, fashion-shop assistant.

Which of these statements most applies to you?
a I am often complimented on my good taste.
b Music is important to me.
c Art is very important to me.

a *You are creative, imaginative, a perfectionist, quite sociable.*
The job for you: photographer, actor/actress, fashion/interior designer.

b *You are self-motivated, happy on your own, want to improve yourself.*
The job for you: musician, record producer, dancer, song-writer.

c *You are thoughtful, artistic, moody, like to be alone.*
The job for you: artist, poet, art/film critic, illustrator.

Which of these statements most applies to you?
a I love money.
b I want to earn a lot.
c I'm bound to earn lots of money.

a *You are calm, logical, like numbers and money, persuasive.*
The job for you: car dealer, salesperson, bank manager, business person, insurance broker.

b *You are cool-headed, smooth-talking, selfish, want power.*
The job for you: estate agent, pilot, travel agent, solicitor, journalist, shop manager.

c *You are ambitious, competitive, ruthless.*
The job for you: newspaper editor, MP, record industry boss, company director.

Which of these statements most applies to you?
a I like to feel useful.
b I like to feel needed.
c I like people.

a *You are hard-working, calm, not very ambitious, sociable, trustworthy, efficient.*
The job for you: firefighter, police, store detective, beautician, personal secretary, social worker.

b *You are caring, optimistic, calm. like people, cheerful.*
The job for you: nurse, doctor, physiotherapist, undertaker, counsellor, speech therapist.

c *You are sociable, relaxed, helpful, great company.*
The job for you: flight attendant, hotel worker, disc jockey, receptionist, shop assistant, bar worker, social worker.

Which of these statements most applies to you?
a I love the open air and moving from place to place.
b I've got a lot of get-up-and-go.
c I like to use my talents in a practical way.

a *You are adventurous, nature-loving, hard-working, a bit claustrophobic*
The job for you: farmer, builder, tourist guide, messenger.

b *You are lively, athletic, competitive, disciplined.*
The job for you: athlete, jockey, sports teacher, army officer.

c *You are efficient, responsible, like animals, single-minded.*
The job for you: vet, environmentalist, police officer, mechanic, surveyor.

Which of these statements applies most to you?
a I'm always doing sums in my head.
b I concentrate better when I work alone.
c I spend a lot of time deep in thought.

a *You are logical, a great student, fast-thinking, good at maths.*
The job for you: accountant, statistician, computer analyst.

b *You are careful, logical, better working alone.*
The job for you: computer operator, engineer, driving instructor.

c *You are practical, scientific, good at concentrating, like being alone.*
The job for you: pharmacist, science teacher, radiologist, electrician, plumber, dentist.

7

Talk to the other students in your group. Do you all agree with the chart? Is it the same as the job you chose for yourself in Activity 4?

Language Summary

Adjective formation from nouns
  Would you describe yourself as **confident**?

-*ing* form and infinitive with verbs of preference
  I **love to work** closely with others.
  Would you like to spend a lot of time in the company of animals?
  You **like being** alone.

see practice page 69

Homework

Choose a student from the group you talked to in Activity 7. Write a paragraph about them. Say which job you think they would be good at and why. Think about their personality, and their answers to the job maze.

Lesson 2 *Can you judge by appearances?*

Language focus:	Present perfect simple and present perfect continuous
Skills focus:	Reading for detail Speaking: asking questions

1

Look at the jobs below and decide which of them are usually done by men and which by women. Compare your ideas with another student.

*barrister doctor editor farmer hairdresser optician
sales assistant   secretary   train driver   undertaker*

2

Listen to Liz telling a story about her job and answer the questions.

1 What was Liz's job?
2 Who did she have to interview?
3 How was she going to travel?
4 Why was she delayed?
5 What was the reason for the mistake?
6 What have you got to do next?

3

Look at these women and try to guess what they do. They all do one of the jobs listed in Activity 1.

Compare your answers with the rest of the class. Ask your teacher to find out if you were right.

4

Read the interview with the doctor. Are these statements true or false?

1 She used to be bald.
2 When patients see her for the first time they worry that she isn't a good doctor.
3 She doesn't think medical training helps doctors communicate with patients.
4 She also wants to be a bus driver.
5 She wants to have a big family.

1 The doctor
'People are surprised that I'm a doctor, and at first they think that I probably can't do the job properly. Most people's idea of a "real" doctor is a slightly overweight man of about 40 – 50 years old. I'm young, I've got my nose pierced and I used to have my head shaved. But if I show that I can do the job, I'm accepted quickly.

'I don't think medical training broadens people's ideas, I think it narrows them. Most people who are accepted for training are middle class, so immediately there is a communication problem. We only had one week out of five years' training about communication skills. I am going to be a general practitioner, so I think it's important to have experience in jobs outside medicine. I've been working with a charity for a long time, and I was a bus driver for a while, too.

'At the moment I live with four medical students. I'd like to live with people who have children, but I don't want any children of my own.'

5

Look at the questions below. Read all the texts and see how quickly you can find the answers.

2 The hairdresser
'I've been a hairdresser for over 20 years and it's what I've wanted to do since I was about sixteen. I've worked with Vidal Sassoon since 1980 and I love it. I'm the only Polish hairdresser here as it's not easy to get permission to work.

'I work part time and my mother-in-law, who has been living with us for about two years, looks after my three sons aged six, four and two.

'I come from Krakow and I've lived in England since 1976. I don't want to go back to Poland because we've been living here too long and all my friends are here. It's great for my children as they are bilingual.'

3 The farmer
'If I go to a party and say I'm a farmer, people are gob-smacked. Then they think I put on my green wellies about once a week and just walk about looking at things – they can't believe I get dirty. If they looked at my hands they would see that I do work with them.

'I've been farming for three years – since Dad asked me to help him. Once I began I got interested.

'In this job I don't meet many people, so I decided to put an advertisement in a newspaper. "Glamorous Female Farmer is looking for intelligent, good-looking man!" I wrote. I've met about twenty men so far.'

4 The sales assistant
'I've worked in a department store for six months now. Before that I worked in an office for three months but I hated it. There was so much paperwork.

'I was so unhappy that I applied for a job as a sales assistant, and got it. When my dad found out he was horrified!

'People think that sales assistants are bored by their jobs, but that's not true. You have to be organized and able to get on well with people. There are training courses too. I've just been on one and I'm going to be promoted soon.'

5 The barrister
'I've been a barrister for five years. People don't believe I'm a barrister because barristers are not usually young, black women. Because I'm young and black, people expect me to have three kids and live in a high-rise flat in London.

'When you work in law you find there is a lot of prejudice about sex and race. I think law is one of the most old fashioned professions you can go into.

'In the future I'd like to continue law and do some fashion design. I want to write, too. I've lived here in England all my life, but I'd like to tell the story of my parents coming to Britain from Guyana, and also continue with writing poetry – I've had some poetry published already.'

6 The train driver
'I remember the first time I walked into the British Rail Dining Room: there were all these men and they all went quiet. They had never had women working there before. I wanted to run away! But everything's OK now, I'm used to it.

'A lot of people think I must get a lot of sexual discrimination and harassment, but I've never really had any of that and the other drivers are wonderful. I've had a couple of passengers knock on the window and say "You're not driving, are you? I think I'll wait for the next one." But you also get people saying "Well done! A woman driver – nice to see." '

1 Who has a ring through her nose?
2 Whose hands will tell you what she does?
3 Who made a whole dining room full of people go silent?
4 Who finds she has difficulties at work because of who she is?
5 Who has wanted to do this job since she was sixteen?
6 Whose children are bilingual?
7 Who works with her family?
8 Whose father was upset when she got this job?
9 Who hated office work?

6

Find these words and expressions in the texts and match them with the correct definition.

1 gob-smacked
(text 3)
  a hit in the mouth
  b very surprised
  c very unhappy

2 wellies
(text 3)
  a rubber boots
  b rubber gloves
  c rubber plants

3 paperwork
(text 4)
  a writing reports and other documents
  b writing newspaper articles
  c making things out of paper

4 a high-rise flat
(text 5)
  a an expensive flat
  b a flat for rich people
  c a flat in a tall building

5 harassment
(text 6)
  a getting into trouble
  b worrying somebody continually
  c getting angry

7

Work in pairs. Choose one or two of the texts and write four questions about them. Then give the questions to another pair to answer.

Homework

Interview somebody about their job. Find out why they chose it, how they feel about it and what they hope to do in the future. Write a paragraph about them.

Language Summary

Present perfect simple and present perfect continuous
  I**'ve lived** here all my life.
  I**'ve been working** with a charity for a long time.

for and *since*
  I've been farming **for** three years, **since** Dad asked me to help him.

see practice page 70

Lesson 3 *Career counsellors*

Language focus: Modal verbs of obligation and advice

Skills focus: Speaking: roleplaying a careers interview
Listening for detail

1

This is David. What do you think he is like? In pairs, write three adjectives to describe his personality.

What do you think he does?

Example

> I think he looks like a travel agent, or maybe a tour guide because he's got a good tan.

> I don't think he works in an office because he's not wearing a suit.

🔊 Listen to David talking to a career counsellor. What does he do? Were you right?

2

🔊 Now listen again and complete the career counsellor's information card about David.

Name: *David Macintosh*

Age:

Qualifications:

Personality:

Previous jobs:

Present job:

Job preferences:

Recommendations:

3

🔊 What are the questions which the career counsellor asks David? Listen again and write down the exact words.

4

Roleplay
Half the class are careers counsellors and the other half are clients who want careers advice. The clients have appointments with three counsellors. Each appointment lasts for three minutes.

Counsellors

Find out as much as you can about your client. At the end of the interview, try to recommend a job for your client.

Use the questions the counsellor asked David to help you.

Write an information card like David's for each client you see.

Clients

Choose one of the photographs on the next page and fill in an information card about them. Write as much detail as possible. Look at the information card about David in Activity 2 to help you.

You are the person on the card you have filled in. You are going to see the counsellors. Answer the counsellors' questions as the person on the card NOT as yourself.

Make a note of the recommendations each counsellor makes. You will need the notes at the end of the roleplay.

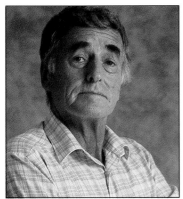

Jorge

Sylvia

Jean-Luc

Bill

Kazuko

Heidi

5

Now form two groups: counsellors and clients.

Counsellors

Find out about the jobs you all recommended to each client, and give your reasons.

Examples

> Really? I thought he would be a good salesperson.

> I recommended that Jorge should be a doctor.

Clients

Discuss who you thought gave the best advice, and give your reasons.

Example

> Carlo told me Sylvia should try a career in television, but I think she'd hate it!

Choose a spokesperson from each group to report your findings to the class.

Homework

Choose a famous person and fill in an information card about them. Think about what they have done in their life, their personality and why they are successful.

When you have completed the card, use the information to write a paragraph about this person.

Language Summary

Modal verbs of obligation and advice
You **have to** have a university degree.
You **must** be good at dealing with people.
You **should** apply in writing.
You **needn't** have a specific qualification.
You **don't have to** have a teaching qualification.

see practice page 71

Lesson 1 *The future of fashion*

Language focus:	Defining relative clauses
Skills focus:	Reading for specific information, predicting Listening to complete a table

1

Match the pictures with the names of the clothes.

1 a sweatshirt ___*d*___
2 a sweatshirt with logo _____
3 tights _____
4 ski-wear _____
5 thermal underwear _____
6 cycling shorts _____

Do you have any of these clothes? Work in pairs and describe your favourite clothes to your partner. Are they in fashion at the moment?

2

Look at this headline:

FASHION FINDS FUTURE IN 'INTELLIGENT' FABRIC

What do you think it means? With a partner, choose from the ideas below:

– clothes that never need washing
– clothes that change colour
– clothes that never wear out

Read the article quickly to find out if you were right.

3

The paragraphs in the article are numbered. Match the paragraphs with the headings.

1 Healthy clothes _____
2 Ski-wear development _____
3 Fashion and temperature _____
4 Why changes are important _____
5 Sweet-smelling underwear _____
6 Fashion in the future _____

1 Fashion is moving into the twenty-first century. A coat that changes colour with the weather; shirt stripes which disappear while you are wearing it; an odour-free blouse that can be worn for days and days... These are not sci-fi fantasies, but the most recent developments in the fashion world, made possible by advances in fibre technology.

2 Jackets by Stone Island change colour in warm weather and cost between £400 and £500. Peter Siddell, a store buyer says: 'There's not much more designers can do with clothes. They need to make new fabrics to keep fashion interesting.'

3 Massimo Osti is the man who has brought these unusual fabrics to the shops. Another Osti invention is the sweatshirt which has a logo on the chest which disappears when you breathe on it. Now there is a range of temperature-sensitive leisure-wear for golfers who like to practise in all weathers. As golfers leave the warm clubhouse, their sweaters change from white to a rainbow of colours.

4 Unika, a Japanese firm, has developed a synthetic fibre called Thermotron which changes sunlight into thermal energy and keeps the wearer up to 10°C warmer than ordinary fibres. One ski-wear fabric turns black to absorb sunlight when the temperature drops to below zero, and changes to white above 5°C to reflect the sun.

5 Tights manufacturers in the Far East and Europe have sold many tights which have been impregnated with fragrances and insect repellent. A department store in Britain reports good sales for magnolia-fragranced tights. The fragrance lasts up to three hand-washes.

6 Now there are tights which even contain vitamin C extract, and seaweed essence! What next...?

4

Look at the article again. Find four examples of clothes that change colour. Find two examples of patterns that disappear. Find something that women could wear to protect themselves from mosquitoes.

5

Match these words from the article with the definitions. Use the article to help you.

1 fibre (paragraph 1)
2 odour-free (paragraph 1)
3 fabric (paragraph 2)
4 temperature-sensitive (paragraph 3)
5 synthetic fibre (paragraph 4)
6 fragrance (paragraph 5)

a a pleasant smell
b reacting to temperature
c material made from threads joined together
d threads made of wool, cotton, etc.
e not having a smell, especially an unpleasant smell
f thread which is produced artificially

6

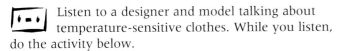 Listen to a designer and model talking about temperature-sensitive clothes. While you listen, do the activity below.

1 Tick the logo that appears on the model's clothes.

2 Tick the pattern that the model would like to appear on the clothes.

3 Where would the model wear clothes like these? Tick the places.

7

 Listen again and make notes on the chart of the advantages and disadvantages of the new fashion ideas.

Advantages	Disadvantages
attracts people's attention	

8

Work in groups and discuss these questions.

1 Which of the new fashion ideas in the article would you like for your clothes?
2 There are always new fashions to make you spend money. Do you think that this is right? Do you think this encourages people to get into debt?
3 What other problems can there be if you try to follow fashion?
4 How fashion-conscious do you think you are?

Language Summary

Defining relative clauses

A coat **that changes colour with the weather**.

Massimo Osti is the man **who has brought these fabrics to the shops**.

see practice page 72

Homework

You are a journalist for a fashion magazine. Your editor has asked you to write a 100-word article about the new fashion ideas. It must consist of three paragraphs and a headline and it must include the following details:

1 colour changes and patterns
2 vitamins, fragrance and insect repellent in fabric
3 advantages and disadvantages of the new developments

Use the information from the newspaper article and the radio programme to help you.

Lesson 2 *Homes*

Language focus: Open conditionals

Skills focus: Speaking: an information gap activity
Listening: labelling a diagram

1

Work in groups of three. You have one minute to write
down as many different types of houses as you can think
of. The group with the largest list should read it to the class.

2

Stuart Bexon has a very unusual house. Here is a
picture of the outside of the house, and a cross-section.

This article in the local newspaper was written
about his house. Work in pairs. Read the article
and answer the questions.

1 Why did Mr Bexon build a house like this?

2 Is this the first time a house like this has been
built?

3 Name one of the problems you might find
with this kind of house.

4 What are the advantages of a house like this?

5 How does Mr Bexon feel about his home?

If you can't go up, go down! When
Stuart Bexon was told he couldn't
build a house on his field in the
village of Westonbirt in the west
of England, he decided to bury his
dream house instead.

Now Bexon is using 600 square
metres of underground living
space. It has three bedrooms, two
bathrooms, a study, kitchen and
dining room and a sunken
swimming pool underneath glass
domes to let in light.

The only part you can see from
the road is the doorway with two
giant doors.

'My idea was to build a normal
house. I was refused permission
because this area has such
beautiful countryside, so I decided
to build my house underground,'
Mr Bexon says.

Bexon was advised by an
architect, Arthur Quarmby,
Britain's leading expert on 'earth
shelters'. Quarmby's own home is
underground.

'I spent a long time talking to
him,' Bexon remembers. 'Quarmby
was very interested, and was able
to pass on useful tips, because if
you build underground, you have
to cope with damp and also keep to
building regulations.'

The problem of lighting the
house was solved by the domes. If
there aren't any windows in the
house, you need to use the ceilings
as windows.

'If you don't have to worry
about the outside of a house, you
have more money to spend on the
inside. The house wasn't really
any more expensive than a
normal one.'

Bexon has used the soil which
was removed to start a gardening
business, and he also now works
as a builder. 'I always wanted to
build my own home, so I found the
work very interesting. If, like me,
you are afraid of heights, being
able to work underground is much
better.'

3

Look at the list of the rooms that Mr Bexon has in his house. Listen to him showing someone round the house and label the plan.

bathroom   bedroom with en suite bathroom
day room   dining room   garage
guest bedroom   kitchen
living room   observatory
study   swimming pool
third bedroom

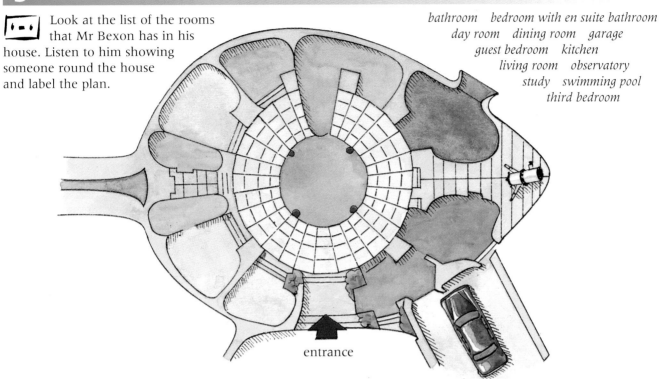

entrance

4

Would you like to live in a subterranean house? Work in pairs. Give your reasons for and against.

5

The rooms in Mr Bexon's house are all different shapes. Imagine you can choose a dream room. Choose one of these shapes for your room:

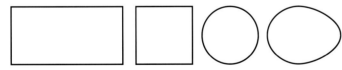

Draw in the furniture and the possessions that are most important to you. You can have eight things.

6

Work in pairs. Do not let your partner see your drawing. Tell your partner what shape your dream room is. Then describe what is in it and where. Your partner must draw a plan.

Tell your partner why you chose the things in your dream room.

Example

Furniture/object	Why you chose it
a big old sofa	Because I love to sit in a comfortable chair when I read.

Homework

Draw a plan of your dream house. Write a description of it. Include

– where it would be
– how many rooms it would have
– what special things you would have in it.

Language Summary

Open conditionals
   If you **can't** go up, **go** down!

Participle adjectives
   Quarmby was very **interested**.
   I found the work very **interesting**.

see practice page 73

Lesson 3 *Advertising and selling things*

Language focus: Intensifiers: very, too, enough

Skills focus: Listening for specific information
Writing descriptions

1

Work in pairs. Look at this riddle. You have three minutes to guess the answer:

With your partner, write a similar riddle. Give it to another pair of students to solve.

> I am small enough to go in your bag, but strong enough to hold your bag together. I am made of paper and plastic. I am cylindrical, but also long and like a ribbon. I am sticky.
> What am I?

2

Read the following advertisements and match the pictures with the descriptions.

1

2

3

4

5

6

a **WIDDINGTON: Very large country house.**
UNFURNISHED accommodation comprises 4 bedrooms, 3 reception rooms, large conservatory, heated swimming pool. Parking for 3 cars. £1,000 p.c.m.

b **WHALE CERAMIC WALL PLAQUE**
An unusual and decorative plaque to put on the wall. Handmade and painted, each plaque is unique.
ref. 009879 £34.00.

c FOR SALE nearly new Amstrad PC 1512, only 4 months old, excellent cond. incl. light pen, twin drives, £450. Tel. 0279 55089.

d SPACIOUS FAMILY HOME
set in quiet location within village. 4 bedrooms, kitchen/breakfast room, c/h, double garage, walled garden. Great Chesterford. £215,000.

e **GREENPEACE RUGBY SHIRT**
A high quality fashioned rugby shirt in unbleached 100% heavyweight cotton. A generous cut allows for 7% shrinkage. ref. 151819
M £22.50; XL £23.00.

f **LOOK INTO THE FUTURE**
with the new 486 66MHz Personal Computer with interactive CD-ROM. Available now from all major retailers.

3

As quickly as you can, look at the advertisements and try to find the answers to the following questions:

1 Which item is handmade?

2 In which house can you go for a swim?

3 Where can you buy the new 486 66MHz personal computer?

4 What sizes of rugby shirt are available?

5 What do you think the following mean?
cond. incl. p.c.m. ref. c/h.

4

How can you describe something you want to sell? With a partner, choose one of the things below and make a word map like this one:

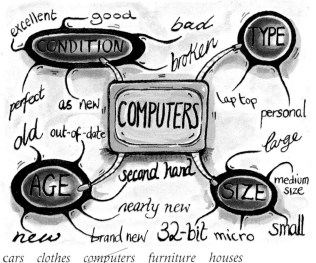

cars clothes computers furniture houses

5

Lesley Johns saw the advertisement for the Amstrad computer in her local newspaper and decided to go and see it. When she arrived she realized that it was not as good as the advertisement had said. Listen to her conversation with the person selling the computer, and complete the table.

features in the advertisement	true	false	correct description
nearly new		✓	*quite old*
4 months old			
excellent condition			
twin drives			
light pen			
bargain			

Homework

You have something you would like to sell. Write an advertisement to place in the local newspaper. Remember to include

- a full description of the object
- the price
- your telephone number or address.

6

Work in pairs. You are selling one of the items in Activity 4. Your partner comes to see it, but it is not the same as the advertisement had said. Discuss the problems in the same way Lesley did in Activity 5.

7

Look at these objects. What information would you include about each one in an advertisement? Work with a partner and write a list.

8

Join another pair and work in groups of four. Write an advertisement for each object. Try to make them sound really attractive.

Show your advertisements to the rest of the class. Which group's advertisements make you want to buy the objects?

Language Summary

Intensifiers
   Very large country house.
   £450 is much **too** expensive.
   It's small **enough** to fit in your bag.

see practice page 74

Lesson 1 *New sports*

Language focus: Modals of deduction

Skills focus: Listening to complete a table
Writing an advertisement

1

Look at this photograph and answer the questions.

1 Who are these people?

2 What are they holding?

3 Why are their eyes protected?

4 What do you think the game involves?

Use these phrases to help you:

*It/They could be...   It/They can't be...   Perhaps...
It/They must be...   It seems to me that...*

Example

They could
be soldiers.

2

Label the photograph using these words.

a belt
b gas canisters
c holster
d marshals
e mask
f paintballs
g pistol
h team armband

3

Work in pairs. These pictures are of some more unusual sports. Look at the pictures and answer these questions.

1 Which sports are they? Choose from this list:
  a abseiling   **e** rock climbing
  b bungee jumping **f** squash
  c gliding   **g** underwater tennis
  d parachuting   **h** white water rafting

2 What do you think happens in each sport?

3 Which of these sports do you think is the most dangerous?

4 Which of these sports do you think needs the most skill?

4

Listen to three people talking about their favourite sport. Which of the sports from page 24 do they do? Compare your answers with a partner.

1 Carl _____

2 Shaun _____

3 Karen _____

5

Now work in groups of three. Each person in the group must listen carefully to one of the people talking and fill in the table for that person.

Then work together in your group and complete your table.

	Carl	Shaun	Karen
Cost			
Equipment			
Training			
How many people take part?			
Where do you do it?			
What happens?			
Why does he/she like it?			

Homework

Write a description of the sport your partner told you about in Activity 9.

6

In your groups, discuss the following questions:

1 Would you like to try any of these sports? Why? Why not?

2 Do people play these sports in your country?

3 What other new or unusual sports do you know about?

7

Here is an advertisement for paintball. Use your table to fill in the missing information.

CAMPAIGN
PAINTBALL SPORTS
ARE PROUD TO PRESENT
WICKED
PAINTBALL
(NOW OPEN)
Cost only _____ per day,
plus _____ p for each paintball
Cost includes equipment:
goggles, _____ , and _____ .
Bring your friends – maximum _____
people _____ training given .

8

In groups, design an advertisement for one of the other sports you heard about.

9

Work in pairs. Interview your partner about a game they play or like. It doesn't have to be an unusual sport. Find out

– where it is played.
– how many people play it.
– the equipment and cost.
– the rules.
– why they like it.

Language Summary

Modals of deduction
   They **could** be soldiers.

see practice page 75

Lesson 2 *The price of fun*

Language focus: Position of adverbs of frequency

Skills focus: Listening to complete a table
Reading for specific information

1

Work in pairs. Look at this picture and write down as many words as you can to describe this place, the people and how you would feel in this place.

Do you enjoy going to these places? What sort of people go there? Why do they go?

2

You are going to hear four young people talking about amusement arcades. First match the following words with their definitions.

1 gamble	**a** money in coins or notes
2 boredom	**b** a job delivering newspapers
3 fruit machine	**c** play games to win money
4 paper round	**d** being bored
5 cash	**e** an informal word for a friend
6 a mate	**f** money given to help students while they are studying
7 a grant	**g** an electronic game – you put money in and if you get three symbols the same you win

3

 Now listen and complete the table.

Name	Age	How often does he/she go there	Why?	Where does he/she get the money from
1 *Philip*				*He's self-employed.*
2	*16*			
3 *Paul Warwick*				
4				

4

Look at the newspaper headline. What do you think an 'Arcade Addict' is? Do you think any of the young people on the tape are arcade addicts? Read the text quickly to find out if you were right.

MISERY OF THE ARCADE ADDICT

Old images of dusty tired men and women as the typical gambling addicts are speedily taking on a new shape, as the problem of young people addicted to fruit machines grows worse.

A suicide note left by John Thompson, aged 23, recorded his miserable fruit machine addiction: 'Fruit machines should be banned, they are bad, bad, bad.' Unable to get their images out of his head he killed himself.

Jacqueline Miller, aged 21, raided a building society to feed her habit, and a 16-year-old stole her mother's jewellery, emptied her own savings account, and spent £500 in one week.

'A lot of it is the flashing lights and the atmosphere and the machines can become an extension of your person,' says Nigel, co-ordinator for Arcade Watch Project which has been set up in Brighton to help young addicts kick their habit.

The Project's aims include carrying out a countrywide information campaign producing educational packs and working actively in amusement arcades to help those who have problems with the machines.

Nigel, who used to be addicted to fruit machines himself, says there are two types of gamblers: those who gamble because they want to, and those who gamble because of a problem at home or school, or with a relationship. Arcade Watch tries to help with informal counselling and group sessions.

'Gambling takes away your confidence, and it's a lonesome activity – kids might go to an arcade with their friends, but they will be playing the machines by themselves. Kids often end up skipping school and stealing to pay for their addiction.'

Michael, aged 13, started gambling when he was 10, getting the cash by shoplifting and selling his own belongings and other people's things. Sarah, 15, spends £30 a day on the machines. 'I lose a lot of money, but they excite me. When I have no money left I feel angry and bad about myself. I hope Arcade Watch can help me.'

Fruit machines are big business – the government received £97,354,000 in licence fees from fruit machines last year, and of course, the arcade owners don't want to recognise the problem.

'We expect to have contact with at least 500 young people a year,' says Nigel. 'Even if we cure just one, then it is one life saved.'

5

Choose the sentence that best summarises the text.

1 Young people who gamble often become addicted to drugs and alcohol.

2 Some young people have problems which cause them to become addicted to gambling: they need help to solve these problems and to avoid other problems.

3 Young people who become addicted to gambling often commit suicide and take drugs because nobody helps them.

4 People of all ages gamble, and need help to avoid the problem.

6

Read the text again and answer these questions:

1 How do the young people in the article get the money to gamble?

2 Why do they gamble?

3 Why is it a 'lonesome activity'?

4 How does Arcade Watch help?

7

The boy who died said 'Fruit machines should be banned, they are bad, bad, bad.' Work in small groups. Decide whether your group agrees with this statement or not. Be prepared to give reasons to the class.

When each group has decided, take a class vote.

Homework

Your friend has started to visit an arcade every day. You are very worried about him/her. Write a letter to your friend telling him/her how dangerous it can be.

Language Summary

Position of adverbs of frequency
Sometimes I do the odd night in a pub.
I **never** play the fruit machines.
I come here almost **every day**.

Present simple for habits and routines
I never **play** the fruit machines.
I usually **come** here after school.

see practice page 76

Lesson 3 *Make your own game*

Language focus:	Defining and non-defining relative clauses
Skills focus:	Listening: a dictation Writing: making a game

1

How good is your general knowledge? Listen to eight general knowledge questions and try to answer them. You will hear them twice.

2

Compare your answers in groups. The group which has the most correct answers is the winner.

3

Here are some cards from a board game:

Work in pairs. To find out how to play the game, you are going to dictate the instructions to each other. Sit back to back.

Student A – look at Dictation A and dictate the first instruction to Student B. Student B – write down instruction 1. Then look at Dictation B and dictate the second instruction to Student A.

Take it in turns to dictate. When you both have all the instructions, compare your texts to make sure they are correct.

Q How many squares are there on a chess board?

Sixty-four A

Q What is the name of the fast food chain which Ray Mac built?

MacDonald's A

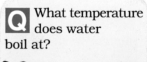
Q What is the name of the smallest continent in the world, which is the home of the Emperor Penguin?

Antarctica A

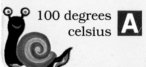
Q What temperature does water boil at?

100 degrees celsius A

Dictation A

1 This game, which is played in pairs, starts by each pair putting their counter on the snail's tail.

2 _____

3 The pair who start must throw the dice and move their counter.

4 _____

5 If the answer is correct, the pair must throw the dice again, move to another square and try to answer the question which the other pair ask.

6 _____

7 The pair who reach home first are the winners!

Dictation B

1 _____

2 Each pair throw the dice. The pair who have the highest number start.

3 _____

4 The next pair must ask a question. The pair who started have 30 seconds to answer the question.

5 _____

6 If they answer incorrectly, the pair who are next to you have to throw the dice.

7 _____

4

Work with your partner. Make ten cards like the cards in Activity 3. In groups of eight or ten students (four or five teams), mix your cards together and follow the instructions to play the game.

Homework

Look at the instructions for this coffee maker. Choose four things which you use regularly and write the instructions for them.

Example

Boil some water. Put four spoonfuls of coffee into the jug. Pour on the boiling water and stir. Wait for five minutes. Push the top down. Pour the coffee into some cups and serve.

Language Summary

Defining and non-defining relative clauses
   The pair **who** start must throw the dice and move their counter.
   What is the name of the smallest continent in the world, **which** is the home of the Emperor penguin?

see practice page 77

Lesson 1 *A mystery*

Language focus: Time linkers

Skills focus: Reading: intensive reading
                      Speaking: storytelling

1

Think of two things you are afraid of. Ask other students in the class and find someone who is afraid of the same things.

2

In this Unit you are going to read a short story. It starts with a woman sitting in a dentist's waiting room. Write down adjectives to describe how you feel:

- before going to see the dentist.
- while waiting in the dentist's waiting room.
- as you walk into the dentist's surgery.
- when you leave.

Work in pairs and compare your answers.

3

Before you read the first part of the story, match these words and expressions with the definitions. Use your dictionary if necessary.

1 wrinkled	sang without opening the mouth
2 fidgeting	without any more delay
3 hummed	spoke suddenly
4 burst out	made a noise with the hands to show impatience
5 without further ado	moving in an impatient way
6 drummed his fingers	with lines on the face

4

Read the first part of the story. Do you think the woman feels the same as you do while waiting in the dentist's waiting room?

The small, wrinkled woman sitting in the corner of the dentist's waiting room had been fidgeting for some time. First, she got up and walked around. After that she whistled, and hummed to herself. Meanwhile, the four other occupants of the room sat quietly, looking at her as the minutes ticked by. Suddenly, she looked round at the other four people waiting and burst out: 'Could I go in next? I'm sure something's happened to my husband. He's been in there for absolutely ages!'

5

Work in pairs. Divide the words in the box into the following groups:

dentist	flying	accidents

ambulance drill extraction fare float

gas cylinder helicopter jet plane mishap

refuel rescue stretcher surgery teeth

6

The words in Activity 5 are all in the story. Work in pairs and decide what the story is about. Join another pair and tell them your story.

7

Read the text and answer these questions.

1 Who does Mrs Crisp speak to?
2 What is the dentist doing?
3 What part of the room does the dentist show Mrs Crisp?

'Certainly,' said the next patient very quickly, with a look of relief on his face. Without further ado, Mrs Crisp walked boldly into the dentist's surgery. The dentist, at his desk, was just replacing his phone. He looked up as she walked in and said: 'You must be Mrs Crisp, the wife of my patient.'

'Yes,' she replied angrily. 'Where is he? He's been in here for such a long time.'

When she said this the dentist looked embarrassed and drummed his fingers on the desk. 'Er... there's been a mishap. Nothing serious. You see the open window there...' and he pointed to the wide open window next to the dentist's chair.

8

How do these people feel during the first part of the story? Choose adjectives from the box.

1 Mrs Crisp
2 The next patient
3 The dentist

angry annoyed anxious calm relieved

happy impatient puzzled nervous

satisfied surprised worried

9

 Listen to the next part of the story. Are these statements true or false?

1 Mrs Crisp was pleased.
2 The dentist called the nurse in.
3 The nurse saw Mr Crisp's legs disappearing.
4 The window was near the ground.
5 Mrs Crisp knows where Mr Crisp is now.

Language Summary

Time linkers
First she got up and walked around.
After that she whistled, and hummed to herself.
He looked up **as** she walked in.

see practice page 78

Homework

Write a description of a visit you have made to the dentist's or doctor's. Say how you felt, what happened to you, and describe the attitude of the dentist or doctor. Don't forget to use the adjectives you have learnt in this lesson. Join your ideas together with time linkers from the story – eg *first, meanwhile, when, after that, as,* etc.

Lesson 2 *Adventure*

Language focus: Past simple and past continuous

Skills focus: Reading for main idea
Listening for specific information

1

These are six words from Lesson 1. The letters are mixed up. Work in pairs to find out what the words are.

1 nixsuao	**2** mcla	**3** ramsdresbsae
4 tpiatne	**5** spmhia	**6** isdpernagiap

2

Read the last part of the story from Lesson 1 and the next part. Then look at the statements below.

'Oh no!' Mrs Crisp cried in horror. 'Was my husband really afraid of having his tooth out? Did he start to panic? Did he jump out of the window?' Mrs Crisp looked very upset. She stood in the doorway staring at the window, then at the dentist again, then at the window. 'What happened? What happened?' She looked all round the room but couldn't see Mr Crisp anywhere. The room looked like any normal dentist's surgery. A large chair, lots of white cupboards, and lots of horrible metal instruments.

'I was washing my hands outside when it happened,' replied the dentist, finally, wiping his forehead with a handkerchief. He sank into his chair, looking exhausted. 'When I came in, the nurse was in the room and everything looked the same as it had done before – well, much the same as it does now, in fact. Well, I looked over at the window and saw his legs – that is, your husband's legs, Mrs Crisp – and they were disappearing over the edge. His legs looked all right, Mrs Crisp, but I'm afraid that's all I could see...'

Mrs Crisp hurried over to the window and looked down. The ground was only about one metre below,

and it looked quite soft. But there was no sign of her husband at all. She looked to the right and left: there were a couple of trees, some flowers, then the car park. The Crisp's car was still parked where they had left it. Mrs Crisp turned back to the dentist.

'He couldn't have hurt himself if he had thrown himself out,' she said, puzzled. 'Where is he?'

'He didn't go down, ' said the dentist, 'he went up!'

'What do you mean, up?'

'Well, he wanted to have gas for the extraction and we had to use a new cylinder. But it must have been the wrong type of gas. As he was breathing it in, the nurse said he became very light and she had to hold him down in the chair. Then she smelt the gas herself and it smelt so strange that she let go of your husband. The window was open and he floated out. It gave her such a shock she screamed. That's when I ran in, when I heard her, and as I rushed in, she fainted.'

Mrs Crisp was frantic. 'I'm not worried about her... What about my husband!'

Some of these statements are true and some of them are false. Decide which are true, and cross out the false ones.

1 Mr Crisp was going to have a tooth taken out.

2 Mr Crisp fell out of the window.

3 The nurse fainted.

4 Mr Crisp started to rise out of the chair.

5 Mr Crisp opened the window.

6 The nurse opened the window.

7 The nurse liked the smell of the gas.

8 Mr Crisp floated out of the window.

9 The gas cylinder was new.

10 The gas was the wrong kind.

Now put the true statements in the correct order.

3

Look at the pictures below. They show what happened next, but they are not in the
correct order. Imagine what happened, and use the pictures to tell your partner the story.

Listen to the next part of the story and put the
pictures in the correct order. Compare what
happens with your story.

1 ___*a*___   2 _____   3 _____

4 _____   5 _____   6 _____

4

This is an extract from a report which appeared in the
local newspaper. Unfortunately the report is wrong. Can
you find six differences between the report and what
really happened?

M r Crisp saw the helicopter while he was being
blown towards France. This was a good place to
go because Mr and Mrs Crisp were going there on
holiday. Mr Crisp floated beside a British Airways jet,
and shook his fist at the passengers.

After that had happened, Mr Crisp began to burp,
which made him start to come down near a nudist
camp. He managed to land on a telephone box.

A local farmer took him home and he telephoned
his wife immediately.

5

Work in pairs. Student A – you are Mr Crisp. You are
at the farmer's house. Student B – you are the
dentist. You are at the surgery. Roleplay the
telephone conversation.

Homework

Write the dialogue between Mr Crisp and
the dentist from Activity 5.

Language Summary

Past simple and past continuous
   I **was washing** my hands outside when
   it **happened**.

see practice page 79

Lesson 3 *Homecoming*

Language focus:	Reported speech: Questions and statements
Skills focus:	Speaking: roleplaying an interview Writing a report

1

Work in pairs. You have FIVE MINUTES to write down as much as you can remember about what has happened in the story so far. Your teacher will tell you when to begin.

2

Before you read the next part of the story, look at the dictionary definition below. It tells us how Mrs Crisp is feeling. Is she in a good mood?

grim /grɪm/ *adj* **-mm- 1** cruel, hard, or causing fear: *His expression was grim when he told them they had lost their jobs, the grim news of his death* **2** determined, esp. in spite of fear: *a grim smile* **3** *infml* unpleasant, not cheerful: *What grim weather!* – **grimly** *adv* – **grimness** *n* [U]

3

Read the next part of the story and answer the questions below.

'That's when he rang me,' the dentist said. 'He asked me what the name of the gas I used was so that he can refuel and take off again to Nice and the Riviera in the South of France. He also asked me if you were here. I told him you were and he put the phone down immediately.'

'He did, did he?' said Mrs Crisp, grinding her teeth angrily.

The dentist looked at her sympathetically.

'I gave him the name of the gas he should have had. When he takes that it'll knock him out. The local dentist will then arrange for Mr Crisp to be transported home.'

Mrs Crisp was not happy. 'He'll wish he was still unconscious when I get hold of him,' she muttered grimly as she left.

1 What did Mr Crisp want?
2 What did the dentist do?
3 Why does Mrs Crisp feel the way she does?

4

These pictures show what happened when Mr Crisp came home. Work with a partner and tell the story.

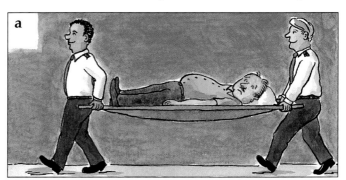
a

b

c

d

 Now listen and check the end of the story.

5

Look at the extract in Activity 3. Underline the way the dentist reports Mr Crisp's questions and reports his reply to Mr Crisp.

This is how we report information. Around the class, take it in turns to report something from the story.

Examples

Mrs Crisp asked the patients in the waiting room if she could go in first.

The dentist told her that Mr Crisp had floated out of the window.

6

The local newspaper is interested in what happened to Mr Crisp and a reporter is going to interview Mr Crisp, Mrs Crisp and the dentist.

Form four groups.

Group A

You are reporters for the local newspaper.

You are going to write a report for your paper. You have to find out exactly what happened, and what people said.
Are all the stories the same?
How did the people involved feel?

Prepare some questions to ask Mr Crisp, Mrs Crisp and the dentist.

Group B

You are Mrs Crisp. You are still angry with your husband.

Tell the reporter what happened and how you felt.

Think about: how the dentist and nurse behaved.
how Mr Crisp behaved.

Prepare your story.

Group C

You are Mr Crisp.

Tell the reporter: about your visit to the dentist.
what happened to you.
how you felt during your adventure.
how you felt when you got home.

Prepare your story.

Group D

You are the dentist.

Tell the reporter: what happened.
how you felt.
how you tried to help.
how you feel about your job now.

Prepare your story.

The interview –
Work in groups of four – Students A, B, C and D.
Student A must now interview the others.

When you have finished the interview, work together to prepare the report. You will all need to take notes to do the homework.

Homework

Write a paragraph for the newspaper, reporting the main events of the story. Give your story a headline.

Language Summary

Reported statements
    I told him you were here.
    The dentist told her that her husband would be unconscious for a while.

Reported questions
    He asked me what the name of the gas was.
    He asked me if you were here.

see practice page 80

Lesson 1 *Hidden secrets*

Language focus: The passive

Skills focus: Listening: ordering information
Reading to complete a text

1

Look at the photograph. What is happening? Where is the dog? What is it looking for?

2

Work in pairs. Look at the following words and phrases to do with Customs. Tick the ones you are sure you already know. Then join another pair and see how many other meanings you know between you.

- ☐ baggage reclaim
- ☐ disguise
- ☐ green channel
- ☐ interrogate
- ☐ prosecute
- ☐ search
- ☐ smuggle
- ☐ sniff
- ☐ suspicious

Check the meanings with your teacher.

3

🔲 You are going to listen to part of a radio programme about the Customs Service at an airport. Listen and answer these questions:

1 What are the Customs Officers looking for?
2 What do they use to help them?
3 Where is the baggage searched?

4

🔲 These are the events which happened at the airport. They are in the wrong order. Put them in the correct order and listen again to check your answers.

1 The customs officer searched the pockets of a pair of jeans.
2 The bag belonged to a scuba diver.
3 A black and white dog was sniffing luggage at the beginning of the conveyor belt.
4 The customs officer searched the man in the customs hall.
5 A dog smelt something in a grey suitcase.
6 Two customs officers took the man to an interrogation room.
7 They found a small amount of marijuana.
8 The dog was interested in a bag.
9 A man of about 26 collected the suitcase from baggage reclaim.

5

You are going to read about some people who smuggle. Half the class will read Text A and half the class will read Text B. Each text has ten gaps. Use the ten words in the box on the next page to complete your text.

Text A

According to a report, women drug (1)_____ account for about 20% of the female prison population, while male drug smugglers make up only 4% of the male prison population.

Maria Lopez de Pisarro is a 42-year-old from South America. On 28 November 1987 she arrived in Britain on a flight from Bogota and was (2)_____. Her baggage was searched and customs officers found several salsa records and children's books. The LPs were examined using an (3)_____ and found to contain (4)_____ of cocaine sandwiched between the vinyl. The books had cocaine (5)_____ in the covers. Maria is now serving a fourteen-year sentence.

'I had a row with my husband and was in Bogota en route for Panama for a holiday. I met someone I knew ages ago, and he offered me a free holiday in Switzerland and asked if I could (6)_____ some books and records to a friend while I was there. I wasn't suspicious at all – they weren't in a sealed suitcase or anything like that. I never even considered they might be drugs.'

Text A continued

A Jamaican woman, Janet Starr, who did know what her suitcase contained, did it for the money and ended up being (7)_____ for seven years. 'I was offered a large amount of money – we needed money: my husband had been out of work for over a year, we have seven children. Eventually the (8)_____ were so great I went to the moneylender. She said she would help me if I took a

(9)_____ of cocaine to London for her. I was shocked, but she said there would be no problems and she offered me £2,000. I didn't realise it would be so dangerous and that I would get such a long (10)_____ if I was caught. Now I am stuck here for seven years – my children send me letters saying 'Dear Mummy, when are you coming back home? We miss you...'

arrested   concealed   convicted   couriers   debts   deliver   parcel   prison sentence   quantities   X-ray

Text B

A common criticism from prison officials and support groups for imprisoned foreign nationals is that most of those arrested as drug (1)_____ are very small players in a far bigger game. The big drugs barons, as they are called, very rarely get arrested.

Hazel Jones, a 45-year-old Jamaican, was searched by customs officers on her return to this country after a stay with her family in Jamaica. They became suspicious after finding a box containing about 30 deep-fried fish cakes in her suitcase. On careful examination by an (2)_____ machine, they found the 'cakes' contained (3)_____ of

cannabis – 13 kilos in all. Like many women in her position, Hazel disclaims all knowledge. 'It was a (4)_____ a friend gave me to deliver in London. He said the contact was a relation of his and was fond of Jamaican fish cakes. How was I to know?' She was (5)_____ and is currently serving a six-year (6)_____.

Jefferson Higgins is a slightly different case. He had financial problems and (7)_____ of almost £10,000. 'I had been gambling heavily for years and it seemed the easy way out. A man approached me when I was on holiday and offered me a large amount of money to (8)_____ a small box to someone in London. I didn't know that it contained heroin, but I thought it was something like that. It seemed easy. I (9)_____ it in the lining of my bag, where I didn't think anyone would find it. I was (10)_____ as soon as I came into the country. I guess I was stupid, but I really thought I'd get away with it.' Jefferson leaves prison in three months' time. He has served four years of a seven-year sentence. He'll still owe the £10,000 when he gets out.

6

Work with a student who has read the other text, and answer the questions for each person: Maria, Janet, Hazel and Jefferson.

1 Why did she/he smuggle?

2 What did she/he smuggle?

3 What prison sentence did she/he get?

Homework

Read the text you didn't read in class and do the vocabulary activity.

Write a newspaper article of about 100 words about a drug smuggler arriving at an airport and being caught. Use these words in your article:

arrested baggage concealed searched smuggle suspicious

7

Do you think all four people should be given the same prison sentences? What are the differences in their cases? Should all drug smugglers be treated in the same way? Discuss in small groups.

Language Summary

The passive
  Where **is** the baggage **searched**?
  Her baggage **was searched**.
  The books **were examined**.
  He **won't be prosecuted**.

see practice page 81

Lesson 2 *Life inside*

Language focus: First conditional

Skills focus: Reading for specific information
Speaking: taking part in a discussion

1

Look at the newspaper headline below. What do you think the article is going to be about? Read the first two paragraphs quickly to find out if you were right.

2

Now read the whole article. As you read, put these headings above the correct paragraphs.

1 What the prisoners think
2 Keeping prisoners out of jail
3 Who pays?
4 Good money
5 High salaries, but a dangerous job
6 Why Chino jail is different

Prison where no one dreams of escaping

1 Behind the barbed-wire fences, gun towers and patrols of armed guards, Chino high-security prison in California, USA, seems like most prisons. However, it's the one jail in the world that people want to get into. Prisoners ask to have their sentences made longer so they can stay there. And when inmates are released they earn more than the police who arrested them.
Why Chino jail is different

2 The reason is a successful rehabilitation scheme that has changed convicts' lives – Chino is the only prison which teaches a deep-sea diving course. While other jails teach inmates how to sew mail-bags, make car number plates or do car repairs, if prisoners are sent to Chino, they will have the chance to become highly-paid commercial divers who will be able to find jobs anywhere in the world.

3 'This course is a life-saver,' says Joe Moore, 25, serving eight years for burglary. 'It's a second chance. If you follow it, it'll give you a skill, adventure and the chance to earn big money.'

4 Inmates leave prison and start jobs where they can quickly earn more than $75,000 a year – much more than prison officers' salaries.

5 'If prisoners follow our programme, they will rarely return to crime,' says Chino's diving instructor, Woodley. 'Only 6% ever come back, while the rest of California's prisoners have a 75% chance of ending up back in jail.'

6 Convicts in Chino have to work hard. If they don't want to work, they should choose to go somewhere else. Only strong people can dive.

7 The scheme has been working for 21 years and has sent divers all over the world, including the Arabian Gulf, the Gulf of Mexico and the Atlantic Ocean.

8 'Diving is a great achievement for inmates,' says Woodley, aged 32. 'It changes their self-esteem and now the course is famous throughout the world. Former inmates have even started their own companies, and come back to Chino to offer work to inmates leaving.

9 Inmates learn how to dive inside two giant five-metre deep tanks which are inside the prison. The prison also has a decompression chamber for treating diving injuries. Other equipment has been given by the US Navy and diving companies. So the course costs less than $9,000 a year.

10 Brian Emery, 31, from California, was convicted six years ago for armed robbery, and he will be released soon. He says, 'Because I've been in prison, employers know I will do a job which other guys won't, either because they're scared or because they don't think the job is good enough. Prison teaches you that if you don't do what you're told, you'll suffer, and you need that in diving.'

11 Tony Charles, 29, from Hawaii, is serving three years for theft and burglary. He has been in prison three times. He says, 'This will be my last time in jail. When I came here I didn't care about anything, but the diving class made me feel proud of myself. Of course I want to earn a lot of money, but I've also really enjoyed the challenge. Unless I do this now, I know I'll return to crime when I get out.'

12 Divers' pay is so good, why don't the prison guards take the course themselves and earn more money?

13 Paul Woodley admits 'I could earn twice as much if I was doing the job I'm teaching the inmates to do, but I'm happy here. I love diving and teaching, but diving is dangerous – you can drown, or suffocate, and many things can go wrong under water.

14 'Because you earn a lot of money being a diver, inmates don't have to rob banks or sell drugs to get money. We're not just teaching people how to dive – we're saving lives.'

3

Read the article again, and answer these questions.

1 Why do the prisoners want to get into the prison?

2 What do prisoners learn in other prisons?

3 When the prisoners leave, what salaries can they earn?

4 How many prisoners return to crime after leaving Chino jail? How many return to crime after leaving other prisons in California?

5 Who provides the facilities for training?

6 Why doesn't the prison guard want to become a diver?

4

Find words or expressions in the text which mean the same as:

1 prisoners (paragraph 1)

2 a programme to teach prisoners to do something useful (paragraph 2)

3 convicted criminals (paragraph 6)

4 success in doing something difficult (paragraph 8)

5 the way people feel about themselves (paragraph 8)

6 people who used to be in prison (paragraph 8)

7 die in water (paragraph 13)

8 die because there is no air (paragraph 13)

Homework

The statements in Activity 5 appeared in a newspaper article about prisons. Write a letter to the newspaper about one of the statements and give your opinion.

5

Work in groups. Look at these statements. Do you agree or disagree with them? Why?

> Prisons like Chino jail are a waste of taxpayers' money. They should train honest people, not criminals.

> It's better to teach prisoners something useful so when they leave prison they can start work immediately. If you don't educate them, they'll just return to crime.

> Convicts have committed a crime. They should be punished, not helped.

Report your group's opinions to the rest of the class.

6

What should a prison be like? In your groups, use your opinions from Activity 5 and make a list of five things a prison should have.

Example

Good training facilities.

Prisoners separated according to their crimes.

Sports facilities.

Language Summary

First conditional
If prisoners are sent to Chino, they **will have** the chance to become highly-paid commercial divers.
If you don't educate them, they**'ll** just **return** to crime.

Revision of *Wh-* questions
Who provides the facilities?
Where will prisoners work?

see practice page 82

Lesson 3 *Punishment*

Language focus: Present perfect and past simple

Skills focus: Listening: intensive listening
Speaking: Making decisions in groups

1

You have one minute to write down as many crimes as you can think of. Who has got the longest list?

2

 Listen to two people discussing a crime they have read about.

1 What has Mark Thompson done?
2 What punishment do the speakers think he should get?

3

 Listen again and make notes in the table below.

Name	Mark Thompson
Occupation	
Family	
Crime	
Punishment	
Reasons	

4

 Listen again to the last part of the conversation and fill in the gaps in the dictation.

Man: Well, I think he _____ _____ to prison. Not for very long, maybe a short sentence.

Woman: But if he's in prison, he _____ _____ for a job, and he _____ _____ the same thing again.

Man: Well, perhaps they _____ _____ him a fine. Maybe £50 or something and a suspended sentence.

Woman: I think the store manager _____ _____ him pay for the toys and maybe he _____ _____ put on probation.

5

Work in small groups. Look at this list of crimes and punishments. Decide which MAXIMUM punishment should go with which crime.

crimes	punishments
armed robbery	death penalty
arson	life prison sentence
drink-driving	long prison sentence (10–20 years)
manslaughter	probation
murder	short prison sentence (1–5 years)
rape	suspended prison sentence
shoplifting	fine
smuggling	
theft	

6

Now look at four criminal cases. Each person has pleaded guilty. Your group must decide the punishment for each person.

You can
- give the maximum sentence (see your answers to Activity 5)
- give a lighter sentence
- acquit

Use the expressions in Activity 4 to help you.

Name: Mary Jenson

Occupation: doctor

Family: married, two children

Crime: Dr Jenson gave an overdose to a 75-year-old patient who had cancer. The patient had asked for the overdose. The patient's family have accused the doctor of murder.

Punishment: _____

Reasons: _____

_____

_____

Name: Jack Cumming

Occupation: truck driver

Family: married, four young children

Crime: Mr Cumming was driving his truck after drinking with some friends on his birthday. He was stopped by the police. He has never done this before. He says if he loses his licence he will lose his job and won't be able to support his children.

Punishment: _____

Reasons: _____

_____

_____

Name: Elizabetta Madison

Occupation: housewife

Family: married, three children

Crime: In the last three years Ms Madison has left her husband nine times. Each time she went to a refuge for women whose husbands are violent. On 16th May she phoned the police to say that her husband was hitting her and her children. The police said there was nothing they could do. Then they got a call from a neighbour saying they had heard a gunshot. They went to the house and found Mr Madison dead. Ms Madison said: 'I thought he was going to kill the children.'

Punishment: _____

Reasons: _____

_____

_____

Name: Karl Anderson

Occupation: student

Family: none (age 14)

Crime: Karl was in a shopping centre with a group of friends. He stole a pair of expensive sunglasses from one shop and some sweets from another. He has offered to pay for the glasses and sweets. He says his friends made him do it.

Punishment: _____

Reasons: _____

_____

_____

Compare your punishments with the rest of the class. Give reasons for your decisions.

Homework

Choose one of the cases from Activity 6. Write a report describing the punishment and your reasons for giving it.

Language Summary

Present perfect and past simple
He**'s been** unemployed for over 18 months.
A man **has stolen** some toys.
In the last three years Ms Madison **has left** her husband nine times.
He **stole** the toys just before Christmas.

see practice page 83

Lesson 1 *In business*

Language focus:	*used to* + infinitive and *be/get used to* + *-ing* form
Skills focus:	Reading and listening to complete a table

1

Suggest age groups for the following stages in life:

0 – ? babyhood   ? – 13 childhood   13 – ? teenage

? – ? middle age   ? – ? old age

Find another student who has written the same ages.

With your partner, write a list of some of the good points and bad points for each age group. Compare your list with other students.

How do you feel about getting older?

2

With your partner, decide on the best age to:

	age
finish education	_____
start work	_____
get married	_____
have children	_____
retire	_____

3

Look at this picture of James Harries who is 13 years old.

1 What do you think James is like?
2 What do you think his life is like? (Look carefully at the photograph.)
3 Write down three adjectives to describe him.

4

Read an interview with James' mother to find out if you were right.

1 James has been an antique dealer for several years now, since about the age of ten, and a year ago he opened Bow-Kays, a flower shop. 'He is used to working with flowers now, and is very good at it,' says his mother, Kaye. 'Like antiques, it needs an understanding of beauty. James knows instinctively when something is valuable.

2 'He buys most things from second-hand sales – we go to about six every Saturday. He can spot anything of value from the queue outside. Eight years ago, when he was only five, he bought Sylvia for five pence. Sylvia is worth £4,000 and is a Royal Doulton statuette. Last year he bought a bag of 'junk' jewellery for 10 pence that contained an antique gold necklace. He sold it two days later for £8,000. At the moment he earns about £200–£300 a week.

3 'We've always had our own business and he has picked up some ideas from us, but he runs his business as he wishes: we don't interfere. His father doesn't think of him as a child any more and I think I'm getting used to treating him as an adult now.

4 'The main problem James has is overcoming the customer's initial surprise that he isn't an adult. But they soon get used to the idea and he usually has them on his side. When he meets someone for a business lunch and he walks into the restaurant and shakes their hand, they stand there with their mouths open. Then they think that he'll probably want a few chips for lunch, but he says, 'I'll have a prawn cocktail and a small steak please'; they're meant to be having a business meeting, but all they're doing is staring at James eating his prawn cocktail!

5 'James used to go to school. He went for about eight years, but he hated it, so we took him out of school a year ago, and now he has four hours of classes a week from a retired headmaster, Lionel Fanthorpe. Lionel says he has never met a boy like James. Usually Mr Fanthorpe thinks that all children should go to school, but he feels that James is so unusual that it would be impossible for him to make progress there.

6 'James is used to hard work, and works as hard at his studies as he does at his business. If he runs out of work he rings Lionel up for more. He is using what he learns to improve his business.

7 'James is very polite. If someone swears during a conversation he will stop talking to them. We really don't know where he gets it from. His father and I used to run a pub, so we're used to all sorts.'

5

Find words in the text which mean the same as:

1 very old valuable objects (paragraph 1)

2 see (paragraph 2)

3 old, useless things (paragraph 2)

4 learnt (paragraph 3)

5 try to be involved in something which has nothing to do with you (paragraph 3)

6 no longer at work because of age (paragraph 5)

7 uses bad words (paragraph 7)

6

Read the interview again, and make as many notes as you can in the table about James.

Education	
Clothes	
Antiques	
Flowers	
Hobbies	
Sports	
Relationships with family	
Relationships with children his age	
Relationships with adults	
Ambitions for the future	

7

 Now listen to James talking about himself and make more notes to complete the table.

8

Work in groups. Discuss these questions.

1 Did you like James? Why? Why not?

2 Do you think he is missing anything in his life?

3 What do you think his future life will be like?

Homework

Write about someone in your family, in the same way James' mother described James. Include a physical description, a character description, information about family, hobbies and ambitions.

Language Summary

used to + infinitive and *be/get used to* + -*ing* form
    His father and I **used to run** a pub.
    I'm getting used to treating him as an adult.
    We**'re used to** all sorts.

ago and *for*
    A year **ago** he opened Bow-Kays.
    He's been an antique dealer **for** several years.

see practice page 84

Lesson 2 *In control*

Language focus: Comparatives and superlatives

Skills focus: Speaking: fluency
                     Reading for specific information,
                     predicting

1

How much control should parents have over their children's lives? Read the statements below, and tick the ones you agree with.

1 Parents should help children with their homework.

2 Parents should be angry if their children don't do well at school.

3 Parents shouldn't mind if their children don't do well at school.

4 Parents should make their children have music lessons.

5 Parents should always want their children to be the best in the class.

6 If their children are happy, that should be enough for parents.

7 Parents should not let their children go out in the evening until their homework is finished.

8 Parents should only allow children to eat sweets at the weekend.

9 Parents should do a lot of sporting activities with their children.

10 Parents should always welcome their children's friends at their home.

Discuss your answers in pairs. Do you think parents should be strict, or not? What happens in your family?

2

Here are the first words of each paragraph of a newspaper article. With a partner, discuss what you think the article will be about.

T hree-year-old Mikhail Marinovich's day starts at 7am with a drink of pureed parsley, carrots, broccoli and spinach...

Mikhail's father, Marv...

Marv is convinced that...

He insists that his children...

Mikhail always eats a lot of protein...

3

Read the article to find out if you guessed correctly.

T hree-year-old Mikhail Marinovich's day starts at 7am with a drink of pureed parsley, carrots, broccoli and spinach. He brushes his teeth, moving the brush alternately with right and left hands.

Breakfast, which is later than most people would eat it (and a lot bigger), is three eggs, unpasteurised skimmed milk, fruit and vitamin supplements. Mikhail again uses both hands alternately.

Mikhail's father, Marv Marinovich, who runs the Performance Training Institute at Anaheim, California, is 52 and on his second family. His first son, Todd, now 21, followed an even more rigorous health and fitness programme throughout childhood and, standing at 1m 95cms of solid muscle, is fast becoming an American football star.

The same plan lies ahead for Mikhail.

Marv is convinced that the greatest athletes are not just born, but can be made. Todd is proof, and Mikhail, he hopes, will be confirmation.

He insists that his children are happy. 'For Todd the whole thing was fun – he needed a more challenging programme than most kids. Mikhail thinks the programme consists of lots of little games which he loves to play.' The 'games' start after breakfast and usually last for three hours. The morning is divided between co-ordination exercises and watching educational TV programmes.

If Mikhail gets unhappy, he's allowed a fruit toast snack. 'He thinks they're candies,' says Marv. 'He's never had real candies.'

Mikhail always eats a lot of protein in the form of eggs, low-fat cheese, tuna, chicken, yoghurt and a minimal amount of red meat. He is not allowed fizzy drinks, milkshakes, sweets and hamburgers. 'This is a much healthier way of eating,' says his father. 'In fact, I believe it is the healthiest programme for a growing child. Without the proper nutrients for your body, you destroy everything you have been doing in the gym.'

4

Read the article again, and answer these questions.

1 What kind of food does Mikhail eat?
2 What can't Mikhail eat?
3 Why does Mikhail have a special diet?
4 Why and when does he play 'games'?
5 Who decides Mikhail's exercise programme and diet?
6 How do we know that Mikhail is happy?
7 Who is Todd? What does he look like? What does he do?

5

In paragraph 4 of the newspaper article, Mikhail's father says he is 'convinced that the greatest athletes are not just born, but can be made'. Work in groups and discuss these questions.

1 Do you agree with what Mikhail's father says?
2 Could you have become a great athlete if you had followed the same programme as Mikhail?
3 Would you have wanted to do this?
4 Are there any problems with a programme like Mikhail's?

Homework

Interview a young person about the control their parents have over their life. Then interview an adult who is a parent. Ask about how much control they have over their child or children. Use the statements in Activity 1 to help you.

Write a paragraph of 100 words about your results.

6

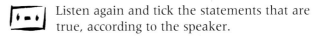 Listen to a child care expert talking about children and sport. Does he think that Marv's programme is a good idea? Why/Why not?

7

Listen again and tick the statements that are true, according to the speaker.

1 Some American children are very overweight.
2 Children who do too much sport can damage their bones.
3 You cannot damage your muscles when you are young.
4 Experts agree that Mikhail's programme is OK.
5 Todd is very rich.
6 Todd's life is like everyone else's.
7 If Todd's football career finishes when he is young, he will be able to get another job easily.

8

Work in pairs. Write five statements FOR this kind of exercise and diet programme and five statements AGAINST it. Compare your statements with another pair.

For

Your country will do better in the Olympic Games.

Against

Children could find making friends more difficult.

Language Summary

Comparatives and superlatives
This is a much **healthier** way of eating.
The **greatest** athletes are not just born, but can be made.

see practice page 85

Lesson 3 *Courting tragedy*

Language focus: Linking words

Skills focus: Listening to complete a table
Writing a letter giving advice

1

Look at this list of words. Put them under the correct headings in the table.

anxiety break bruise cartilage cut depression
elbow fracture knee leg ligament muscle
sprain stress tension

injuries	parts of the body	psychological problems
break		*anxiety*

Check your list with another student.

2

This is Monica Seles. What sport does she play? Why is she holding a cup? Discuss your ideas with a partner, then ask your teacher for the answers.

3

Work with your partner. What do you think the lives of tennis stars are like when they are young and preparing for success? Make some notes.

Examples

> They have to practise all the time.
> They have to get up very early.

Listen to a tennis coach talking about young tennis players. Look at your notes. Does the tennis coach mention any of your points?

4

Listen again, and make notes in the table about the four tennis players.

Tracy Austin
successes
physical problems
life now
Jennifer Capriati
family
school
Monica Seles
early life
family relationships
Hana Mandlikova
relationships

5

Listen to the rest of the interview. What advice does the tennis coach give to young sportswomen? Do you agree with the advice? Discuss with a partner.

6

Half the class read Letter A below and half the class read Letter B. Who is your letter from? What is the problem?

7

Work in pairs with someone who has read the same letter. You work for a magazine problem page. With your partner, write a reply to the letter, giving advice.

When everyone has finished, join another pair from the other half of the class and exchange your replies. Read the other pair's letter and their reply. Do you agree with their advice? Discuss your opinions in your group, then with the whole class.

Letter A

Dear Auntie Pat

I don't know what to do. I am a good swimmer and I love it. I want to do well, and I know I can. I spend five hours every day training – before and after school – and at weekends I take part in competitions. I've always enjoyed it, until recently. The problem is that although I love spending my time training, I'm 15 years old, and I don't really have any friends because all I do is swim. My parents support me and encourage me, but yesterday I had a terrible row with my father and I told him I don't care if I never swim again!

Although that's not really true, I'm very unhappy. What should I do?

'Fed-up daughter'

Letter B

Dear Auntie Pat

What am I going to do about my 15-year-old daughter? She is our only child, and I have always tried to give her everything I never had, and all the encouragement my parents never gave me. I was good at swimming when I was young, but my parents only wanted me to be successful at school.

Angela is also very good at swimming. It has been hard because we don't have much money, but we have encouraged her, and I go everywhere with her, during competitions and training. I have given her all my attention. However, nowadays she is rude, and even tells me to mind my own business. We have also started to have rows, and sometimes I even feel she hates me, whereas I do my best to show her how much I love her.

What can I do?

'Hurt father'

Homework

Write a letter giving advice to either James or his parents (from Lesson 1 in this unit) or Mikhail or Marv (from Lesson 2). Warn them of any possible problems they may have in the future and try to give them advice.

Language Summary

Linking words: conjunctions; contrast, reason and result linkers
   We have **also** started to have rows.
   It has been hard **because** we don't have much money.
   Although I love spending time training, I don't have any friends.
   I feel she hates me **whereas** I do my best to show her I love her.

should and *ought to* for advice
   You **should** try to understand her problems.

see practice page 86

Lesson 1 *Alternative healing*

Language focus: Reported speech: Reporting verbs

Skills focus: Reading a diary for detail
Speaking: comparing and
exchanging information

> Princess Diana
> has it to stop stress; Sylvester Stallone uses it
> to help the skin on his face to stay firm; the Chinese
> use it for everything, and have done for over
> 5,000 years... What is it?

1

Work in small groups. Write down as many facts as you
can about acupuncture.

Listen to this introduction from a radio
programme about acupuncture to find out if
you have the same information.

2

Listen again. Are these statements true or false
according to the speaker?

1 Acupuncture cures you by blocking energy in your body.
2 It doesn't matter where the needles go.
3 Acupuncture is helpful if you can't sleep.
4 Only one needle is used at a time.
5 If you are fat you will have bigger needles.

3

What can you expect?

Below is an extract from
Helen's diary. She is
writing about her visits to
the acupuncturist. Before
you read her diary, look at
the picture of Helen. What
is her problem? What do
you think she has tried to
do about it? Now read an
extract from her diary.
Were you right?

Tuesday 30th April

There doesn't seem to be anything that acupuncture can't
cure! But can it help me to stop the habit I've had for 17 years?
Nail biting! I've tried wearing gloves and that awful no-bite
liquid. I realize that I bite them a lot when I'm nervous and
anxious. Perhaps I should tie my hands to my sides? No good,
I'm desperate! The acupuncture session starts tomorrow...

4

Work in three groups – A, B, and C. Read your diary
extract and answer the questions in your groups.

Wednesday 1st May   Group A

Session 1: I expected some questions but not how many cups of
coffee I drink! She looked at my tongue. Ugh! But a good way to
see if you are healthy. The massage was wonderful, and then came
the needles. Sealed in a foil packet, they were 7 centimetres long.
She used five altogether: one on either side of my right ankle, one
on the inside of my left ankle, and one on each wrist. I didn't feel
much. I soon felt relaxed and my arms seemed to grow and my legs
to get shorter! She admitted that people felt that a lot. After 20
minutes she took the needles out. Result: I felt relaxed for the rest
of the day, but I was biting my nails at the first moment of stress.

Monday 13th May   Group B

Session 2: 12 days later and a different practitioner – the other
one is on holiday. No massage, but lots of questions about my
job. I wanted to explain that I don't just bite my nails at work, I
do it even when I'm doing aerobics! The needles were round my
feet, but this time I had two between my middle and wedding
finger on my right hand. The acupuncturist told me that I would
feel calmer, but I wasn't calm this time and watched the
minutes tick by. Afterwards I told her that I felt uncomfortable.
Result: I bit my nails as I wrote the cheque!

Wednesday 22nd May   Group C

Session 3: (Nine days later) Back to the first practitioner. She
asked me if I had noticed any changes. I said no, but I enjoyed
recording what I ate, how I slept and when I felt stressed.
Looked at my tongue again and then put three needles in my
right foot and one in my right arm – on the inside of the elbow. I
was tense at first, but she moved the needle in my arm and the
difference was extraordinary. I felt sleepy and as though I was
sinking into the couch. Then she advised me to have 10 minutes
rest and I booked another session. I still feel sleepy after two
days and I only started to chew my nails this evening!

1 What questions does the acupuncturist ask Helen?
2 How many needles were used, and where?
3 How did she feel during the session?
4 How did she feel after the session?
5 Did she stop biting her nails?

5

Work with two students who have read the other extracts. Find out if all the sessions were the same. Then answer these questions.

1 What surprised Helen about the sessions?
2 Were they successful?
3 Do you think that Helen will continue to go?

Read the last extract to find out what happened.

Monday 27th May

Still biting my nails, but I realize that any change has to happen over a longer time. Also I realize how helpful it is talking to the acupuncturist. You examine what you eat and talk about your health – so I've decided to stick with it.

6

Work in pairs. Write a mini-questionnaire of five or six questions to ask other students about themselves. Include questions about their habits, (eg smoking, watching too much TV, eating too much chocolate) what they have tried to do to help themselves, and what they think about acupuncture.

Examples

Have you got any bad habits?
What time of day do you find the worst?

Use your questionnaire to interview as many other students in the class as you can.

Homework

Read all of Helen's diary.

Keep your own diary for the next week and record what you ate, how you slept and when you felt stressed.

7

Look at this magazine article about an alternative to acupuncture. Why does it suggest we might prefer this to acupuncture?

Read the article and answer these questions as quickly as you can.

1 Should the pressure from your fingers be strong or weak?
2 How long should you apply the pressure?
3 How should you breathe when you do this?

under pressure

Not up to needles? Our fingertip acupressure tactics could give fast relief from simple health problems.

The ancient Eastern technique of *shiatsu* (literally, 'finger pressure') works on the same principles as acupuncture but uses fingers, rather than needles, to manipulate points. Shiatsu therapist Simon Brown has let us into some trade secrets which you can try yourself.

You should apply quite strong pressure to the point with your fingers or your thumb for about five minutes on each side.

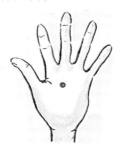

Symptoms Feeling stressed out; overworked
Go for it The Pulse of Weariness
Find it in the centre of your palm (left), below the middle finger

TIP The way you breathe is all-important. Take deep, even breaths while practising acupressure. As you breathe in, relax the pressure; as you breathe out, apply pressure.

8

It is nearly the end of the lesson. How are you feeling? Overworked? Tired? Stressed? Try the exercise in the article with a partner.

Language Summary

Reporting verbs
The acupuncturist **told me** that I would feel calmer.
She **admitted** that a lot of people felt that.
She **advised me** not to go home immediately.

see practice page 87

Lesson 2 *Alternative eating*

Language focus: Past simple and past perfect

Skills focus: Listening to complete a table
Speaking: expressing opinions

1

Look at this cartoon. What do you think the waiter means by 'health foods'? Look at the shopping list below and tick the foods which you think are healthy.

beans	frozen vegetables
bread	lemonade
brown rice	liver
cake	milk
cereal	nuts
cheese	potatoes
coffee	sausages
cream	steak
crisps	tea
fish	white rice
fresh vegetables	yoghurt

Compare your list with other students. Did you all tick the same things? Give reasons for your answers.

2

Write down everything you ate yesterday. How much of what you ate is healthy? Who is the healthiest eater in the class?

3

Many people don't eat meat. They are called vegetarians. Why do you think they don't eat meat? Work in small groups. Make a list of four or five possible reasons.

4

Listen to Kate talking about being a vegetarian. Why did she become a vegetarian? Does she mention any of the reasons on the list you made in Activity 3?

"We used to have a violinist, but now that we're serving health foods ..."

5

Listen again, and make notes under these headings.

Why Kate gave up eating meat	
Why other people give up eating meat	
How Kate feels now	
Other people's attitudes to vegetarians	

6

Work in pairs and answer these questions.

1 Are you a vegetarian?

2 Would you like to be a vegetarian?

3 What is your attitude to vegetarians?

7

Now read this advertisement which encourages people to eat meat. What reasons does it give for not being a vegetarian?

It's not easy keeping a body well-balanced.

- To keep your body well-balanced, you need a huge variety of nutrients every day.
- There's a natural source which contains an abundance of what's good for you.
- This source is full of healthy vitamins, minerals and proteins.

Meat

- Meat provides essential minerals, is vital to healing and enhances our sense of taste.
- All these can greatly increase your health and well-being.

Are you getting enough meat?
The benefits are plentiful.

8

Read the advertisement again, and match these words from the text with their meanings.

1	well-balanced	**a**	advantages
2	nutrients	**b**	without having too much of any one thing
3	source	**c**	elements of food which keep a body healthy
4	abundance	**d**	a large amount, and easy to find
5	well-being	**e**	good general condition
6	benefits	**f**	origin

9

With your partner, make notes in the chart below. Use ideas from the interview with Kate, and from the advertisement, and add your own ideas.

Reasons for being a vegetarian	Reasons for being a meat-eater
for health	*meat is full of vitamins*

10

Roleplay
Work in pairs. Student A – you are a happy vegetarian. Student B – you are a happy meat-eater. You have five minutes to try to convince each other that your way of thinking is the right one.

Homework

Imagine you are planning to open a new restaurant which serves the best of your country's food. Design a menu. Include starters, main courses, desserts and drinks. Give the restaurant a name.

Language Summary

Past simple and past perfect
I **became** a vegetarian six years ago. Before that I **had** always **eaten** meat.
I **decided** one day that I **had eaten** enough meat in my life.

see practice page 88

Lesson 3 *Alternative thinking*

Language focus: Adjective prefixes

Skills focus: Listening: ordering information
Writing a letter requesting information

1

Sit in a comfortable position. Close your eyes and listen to the voice on the tape.

2

Work in pairs. Tell your partner about your special place. Describe what it looked like and how you felt there. Tell them about the thing you brought back with you and explain why you chose it.

3

Choose one word to describe how this activity made you feel. Your teacher will make a list of everyone's words on the board. Are the words mostly positive or negative?

4

Matthew Manning helps people who are seriously ill. He has unusual powers. Listen to Matthew talking about how he discovered his powers. As you listen, tick the adjectives which he uses to describe how he felt.

☐ afraid   ☐ astonished   ☐ astounded

☐ excited   ☐ frightened   ☐ happy

☐ puzzled   ☐ surprised   ☐ terrified

5

This is what happened to Matthew when he was younger. The events are in the wrong order. Try to put the events in the correct order and listen again to check your answers.

1 Four days later it happened again, and Matthew's father thought it was a poltergeist (a ghost which throws things).

2 When Matthew was 11, his father found a silver cup in the middle of the living room.

3 A psychic investigator came and said that Matthew had caused the objects to move.

4 The family always kept the silver cup in a cupboard.

5 Matthew realised that by using these powers he could help people.

6 At school his bed suddenly flung itself into the middle of the room.

7 When Matthew was on holiday from school the strange movements began again.

8 Matthew went to India.

9 Scientists in Canada thought they could help Matthew.

10 Matthew wrote in foreign languages he didn't know.

6

Work in pairs. Write three questions you would like to ask Matthew about his healing powers.

Now read the article below. Does the article answer your questions?

The first person Matthew was asked to treat was a woman who was dying from cancer. Matthew was twenty one. 'I just sat and held her hand and tried to concentrate on expelling the cancer cells,' he says. Nothing happened, but when he returned six hours later, she was sitting up in bed, and she had eaten dinner. He gave her another 'healing' and left.

That night she died. Matthew felt very unhappy about what he had done, so he didn't try to heal anyone else for two years. Then he realised that part of a healer's job is helping patients who know they are going to die. 'Some people think it is unkind or insensitive to say this, but I enjoy helping people die without pain or fear, as well as helping people to live. To me it is just as important. To me, suffering is unnecessary: we all have to learn to accept our fate.'

Matthew's patients are expected to help with their healing. For example, patients with cancer have to think of their unhealthy cells as weak and at the same time to think of the healthy cells as an army who will look after their body and destroy the weak cells. One little girl decided to think of the cancer cells as pieces of cheese and the healthy cells as mice that ate the cheese. When the pain was very bad, she got the mice to the cheese quicker by putting them on motorbikes; the cancer disappeared.

Matthew sees his patients three or four days a week, and the rest of the time he travels around the world giving healing workshops. He has so many patients that there is an eight-month waiting list. Nobody is allowed to change their place on the list, although he might suggest other healers who might help. He has also made some cassette tapes for self-healing.

Matthew says that one thing a person must <u>not</u> be is impatient. Healing takes time and effort to work, and being impatient only causes stress and anxiety which make things worse. What you have to concentrate on is relaxing and thinking positively.

A lot of people are intolerant of alternative healing methods, and want some explanation, but Matthew doesn't try to explain what he does. He knows that there is a strong positive energy, but he doesn't give it a name. He will only say, 'It's the boys and girls upstairs.'

7

Read the article again, and use the information to complete this summary.

Matthew has helped many (1) _____ patients by asking them to visualise the (2) _____ cells destroying (3) _____ He doesn't just help people (4) _____ , he also helps them to (5) _____ and he thinks this is equally important. So many people come to him that he can't help them all himself, so he often refers them to (6) _____ . Matthew can't explain his power, but he says he thinks it comes from (7) _____

Homework

Find an advertisement in a magazine or newspaper for something you are interested in.

Write a similar letter to the one in Activity 9 asking for more information.

8

From the listening and the article about Matthew, choose:

1 One thing which you didn't believe.

2 One thing which surprised you, or which you found strange.

3 One thing which worried you.

Find one other student in the class who has the same answers as you.

Is there anything that all the class feel the same way about?

9

Read this letter which someone has written to Matthew asking for more information. The paragraphs are in the wrong order. Work with another student and put them in the correct order.

> 7 High Street
> Bolton
> Lancs
> 4th September
>
> Mr Manning
> Matthew Manning Centre
> Highbury
> London N5
>
> Dear Mr Manning,
>
> I look forward to hearing from you soon.
>
> I am very interested in your method of helping and healing people who are suffering.
>
> I saw an article in this week's copy of Best about you and your centre.
>
> I would be grateful if you would send me more information about your services, including cost and how to make an appointment.
>
> Yours sincerely,
>
> Erica Aguila

Language Summary

Adjective prefixes
Matthew felt very **un**happy.
Being **im**patient only causes stress.

Articles
The family always kept **the** cup in the cupboard.

see practice page 89

Lesson 1 *Could they be the same person?*

Language focus: *both, neither, either*

Skills focus: Reading for main idea and detail
                      Listening for specific information

1

Work in pairs and discuss these questions.

1 How common are twins?
2 Are they always identical?
3 Are twins always good friends?
4 Can they feel each other's pain?
5 Are twins good at the same things?
6 Do you know any twins?

2

 Listen to Pauline talking about her life with Diana, who is her twin, and answer these questions.

1 Are they identical?
2 Are they close?
3 Did they dress in the same way when they were children?
4 Do they dress in the same way now?

3

Listen to Pauline again, and decide if the sentences below are true or false.

1 Diana was born first.
2 Pauline was a good baby.
3 The twins liked acting.
4 Pauline won two prizes at school.
5 Most people just called them 'twin'.
6 They were jealous of each other.
7 They helped each other in difficult situations.
8 They now have similar jobs.

4

Look at the picture of Clive and Keith Owen. Do you think their relationship is like Pauline and Diana's? Can you tell the difference between them?

Read the article quickly to find out if you are right.

I was to meet Keith and Clive Owen at 1pm in front of Moorgate Tube Station. I had never met them before, but I knew they worked in telephone maintenance. At 1pm two similar-looking men started to work on a pay phone at the station. I was just about to introduce myself when two voices behind me simultaneously called my name.

I turned around and saw a man. Next to him was – the same man! The two wore identical suits, shirts and ties and carried small metal lunch boxes. One of them spoke: 'I'm Keith and this is Clive, or that's Keith and I'm Clive, it doesn't matter.' They laughed and we set off for the pub.

It is very hard to interview Keith and Clive Owen, to remember who said what. On the other hand, it really does not matter as they both say the same things. Ask either of them a question, and the answer will be the same. They finish each other's sentences and say the same things simultaneously. Keith: 'It doesn't matter if you mix us up.' Clive: 'The differences between us are nearly non-existent.' Keith: 'Practically nil.' Clive: 'The same seed, you see.'

Keith and Clive's movements seem beautifully choreographed as they speak. One leans forward to speak as the other leans back. As I ordered beers, I noticed the barman staring at the twins. I asked them what people said when they saw them together. Simultaneously they said: 'Have I been drinking?'

On one occasion, Keith was told that his brother had been injured in a car accident. As Keith rode his motorbike to the hospital, he had to keep stopping because he had pains in his ribs. On arrival at the hospital, he discovered that Clive had broken a number of ribs.

The brothers' medical histories are almost identical. Both had operations at the same time and had their tonsils out together. The prescription for their glasses is identical. For a month in the sixties, the two were laid up with bronchitis – Clive in London and Keith in Nairobi.

Both have recently had stitches placed in exactly the same parts of their mouths; the twins leaned forward to show me – a strangely frightening sight.

5

Read the article again, and answer these questions:

1 What do they do?

2 What do people say when they see Clive and Keith together?

3 Why did Keith have a pain in his ribs?

4 What did the twins show the interviewer that he found strange?

6

Listen to the rest of the interview, and make notes about what happened in the twins' lives next to the dates below.

1932	*twins born in Wales*
1947	_____
1950	_____
1952	_____
1958	_____

Homework

Write a paragraph about your partner's family life. Include information about the family, and about how your partner feels.

7

Why do you think Clive and Keith have a good relationship? Why is Pauline and Diana's relationship more difficult?

8

Find other students in the class who have the same number of brothers and sisters as you. Make a group with these people.

Work in pairs with someone from your group, and discuss these questions.

Questions for students with brothers/sisters:

1 Are you ever lonely or jealous?
2 Do you argue with your sisters/brothers or parents? What about?
3 Do you have the same clothes as your sisters/brothers?
4 Do you have a good relationship with your sisters/brothers?

Questions for students with no brothers/sisters:

1 Are you ever lonely?
2 Do you argue with friends? What about?
3 Are you ever jealous of people with large families?
4 Do you think you have a special relationship with your parents, which people from large families do not have?

Now talk about what you discussed with a student from the other group and make notes. You will need these for your homework.

Language Summary

both, either, neither/nor
We **both** won prizes.
Neither Pauline **nor** Diana liked being a twin.
Ask **either** of them a question, the answer will be the same.

so did..., neither/nor did...
I absolutely hated it and **so did** Diana.
Keith didn't like that and **neither did** Clive.

see practice page 90

Lesson 2 *If you could choose*

Language focus: Second conditional

Skills focus: Listening for main idea and detail
Speaking: giving personal
information

1

Work in pairs. Here are some words which you might use to describe people. Which words do we usually use for men, and which for women?

active aggressive brave clever clinging

emotional gentle handsome kind logical

overpowering powerful pretty quiet

rational ruthless small soft strong tall

tender weak

Ask another pair if they have the same ideas as you.

2

This is the chorus of a poem. Read it and then discuss the questions with your partner.

Ah, but boys will be boys

It's a fact of human nature,

And girls will grow up to be mothers.

1 What special things do only boys do?
2 Do you think all girls want to be mothers?
3 What do you think the rest of the poem will be about?

3

Some of the words in the list below are in the poem. Listen to the first part of the poem and tick the words which you hear.

☐ brother ☐ dirty ☐ dolly ☐ father
☐ friends ☐ Jackie ☐ Janie ☐ jet plane
☐ John ☐ neighbour's gun ☐ noisy
☐ Peter ☐ pretty ☐ screaming ☐ shouting
☐ sister ☐ trouble

4

Work in pairs and listen again. Student A – find out about Janie and describe her. Student B – find out about Peter and describe him. Do you think the poem is correct about young people today?

5

With your partner, listen to the second part of the poem. What has happened to Janie and Peter?

Listen again, and fill in the gaps.

Now what's come over Janie? Janie's turning _____,

Left hook to the _____, right hook to the _____.

Vicious little hussy, now Peter's started bawling,

What a bloody cissy! Who said you could _____?

Because boys _____ be boys,

It's a fact of human nature,

And girls _____ grow up to be mothers.

Now the world's gone topsy-turvy, Janie wants a _____,

And Peter just seems happy _____ prams along,

It makes you feel so _____, kids are such a worry,

_____, _____, tell me, where did we go wrong?

Why does the chorus change from *boys will be boys* to *boys must be boys*? What does the author think about Peter and Janie's behaviour?

8

Work in pairs. If you could live your life again, would you prefer to be male or female?

Listen to four people answering this question, and make notes in the table:

Name	M/F	Why?
Kerry	F	Men can't have babies. Men can't cope on their own.
Rob		
Paula		
Yves		
Your partner		

6

Find words in the second half of the poem which mean the same as:

1 happened to
2 punch using the left hand
3 wanting to hurt someone
4 crying loudly
5 upside-down
6 girl acting in an unfeminine way
7 boy acting in an unmasculine way

9

Ask your partner the following questions and make notes for them.

1 If you could live your life again, would you prefer to be a man or a woman?
2 What are your reasons?
3 In your country, do you think life is easier for a man or a woman?
4 In which countries do you think it is easier to be a woman, and in which countries do you think it is easier to be a man?

7

Look at the following statements in groups. Do you agree with them?

> Boys and girls behave differently because of their upbringing, not their biological make-up.

> It is reasonable for a wife to work while her husband stays at home and does the housework and cares for the children.

> Women want to have equal opportunities, but they don't want to be the same as men.

Homework

Interview at least four other people using the questions above. Use your results to make a table like the one in Activity 8.

Language Summary

Second conditional
If you **could live** your life again, **would** you prefer to be a man or a woman?

see practice page 91

Lesson 3 *Trading places*

Language focus: Conditional clauses without *if*

Skills focus: Listening for detail
Speaking: talking about an imaginary situation

1

These are pictures of ordinary objects, but they look very different. With a partner, try to guess what they are.

Compare your answers with the rest of the class.

2

Look at a dictionary definition of disguise.

disguise² *n* **1** [C] something that is worn to hide who one really is: *Nobody saw through his disguise.* (= nobody recognized him) **2** [U] the state of being DISGUISED: *He went to the party* **in disguise**.

Work in pairs. Read the article quickly to find out what the disguise in the headline is.

MONEY MAKING IN DISGUISE

When Fiona Hatton's mother-in-law became ill with cancer, Ms Hatton did not know very much about the illness.

'My mother-in-law didn't smoke and her diet was good,' says Fiona. 'I went with her to talk to the doctor and it was obvious that the doctor didn't know what had caused her cancer.'

As a result of this, Fiona decided to raise money to build a research centre. The target is £15 million but she expects to get much more.

In a careers analysis, Fiona once scored 95% for persuasiveness – and this proved very helpful in her involvement with Comic Relief and British Film Year, which were both events where the public were persuaded to give money to charities – and they gave more money than people thought possible.

Today the publicity campaign for *Trading places* has begun across the country. On Friday 27th March, hundreds of celebrities and other members of the public will pretend to be someone else for the day: they will dress in their clothes, make themselves look like the other person and do their job.

To find out how you can exchange places with someone else and raise money for Cancer Research, phone 071 445 5511.

3

Read the text again and answer the questions.

1 What made Fiona want to raise money?
2 What is the money for?
3 How much does she hope to raise?
4 What is Fiona very good at?
5 Who is going to take part in *Trading places*?

4

You are going to listen to Dina Rabinovitch who took part in Fiona's campaign. Before you listen, match these words from the listening with their definitions. Use a dictionary if necessary.

1 lipstick
2 unisex
3 a barber
4 sonny
5 a sponsor

a a men's hairdresser
b make-up for your lips
c a familiar name older people sometimes use for young men
d someone who gives you money for doing something
e suitable for both men and women

5

Dina pretended to be a man for the *Trading places* day. With a partner, discuss what you think happened, how people reacted and any problems she might have had.

6

Listen to Dina talking about her day as a man. Were your predictions correct? Listen to the first part of the tape again. How did Dina change her appearance? Write notes in the table.

clothes	bought a suit
hair	
face	
general physical appearance	

7

Listen to the rest of the tape. Dina talks about four main events during the day. Make notes about each event.

in the street	policeman called her 'sonny'
in the men's club	
in the pub	
walking home	

8

Work in pairs. Was there anything that surprised you about Dina's experience? What do you think would happen if you did the same thing in your country?

9

Imagine you are raising money for Cancer Research, and you are going to be somebody else for a day. Work in groups. Tell each other who you would be – eg a famous person, a friend, someone who does a job you would like to do – and why you would like to be this person for a day.

Homework

Imagine you have spent the day as the person you chose in Activity 9. Write about what happened and how you felt.

Language Summary

Conditional sentences without *if*
    Tell each other who you **would** be.

Conditional sentences with other words
    Unless I put my belt on my hips, I wouldn't look aggressive.
    As long as I wore men's clothes, people would treat me differently.

see practice page 92

Lesson 1 *Green is the colour*

Language focus:	Future with *will* and *going to*
Skills focus:	Reading: using information to complete a text
	Writing: making a poster

1

What does the word *green* make you think of? How many objects can you think of which are green? How many different green colours can you think of – eg *dark green, pale green...*?

2

Work in pairs. Look at the photographs. Which of the words in the box go with which picture? Use your dictionary to help you. Some of the words can be used for more than one picture.

> atmosphere   carbon monoxide   chemicals
>
> disposable   dump   factory   fumes
>
> industrial waste   ozone layer   pollutant
>
> pollution   pump   river   rubbish
>
> sewage plant   smog   toxic gases   traffic
>
> ugly   unleaded petrol

3

Listen to Larry talking about one of these problems in his country. Which picture shows the problem he is talking about? As you listen, tick the words you hear him use. Did you choose the same words for this picture?

4

Listen to Larry again, and make notes about –

1 the cause of the problem.
2 what the government is doing to prevent it.

5

Choose one of the pictures and talk to another student about the problem and what your country does about it.

6

Look at the posters on the next page asking people to take more care of the environment. Find two things you do which are good for the environment, and two things you do not do at the moment.

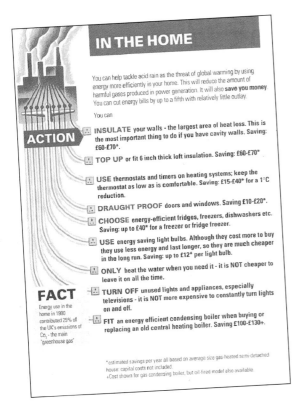

IN THE HOME

You can help tackle acid rain as the threat of global warming by using energy more efficiently in your home. This will reduce the amount of harmful gases produced in power generation. It will also **save you money**. You can cut energy bills by up to a fifth with relatively little outlay.

You can

ACTION

- **INSULATE your walls** - the largest area of heat loss. This is the most important thing to do if you have cavity walls. Saving: £60-£70*.

- **TOP UP or fit 6 inch thick loft insulation. Saving: £60-£70***

- **USE thermostats and timers on heating systems; keep the thermostat as low as is comfortable. Saving: £15-£40* for a 1°C reduction.**

- **DRAUGHT PROOF doors and windows. Saving £10-£20*.**

- **CHOOSE energy-efficient fridges, freezers, dishwashers etc. Saving: up to £40* for a freezer or fridge freezer.**

- **USE energy saving light bulbs.** Although they cost more to buy they use less energy and last longer, so they are much cheaper in the long run. Saving: up to £12* per light bulb.

- **ONLY heat the water when you need it - it is NOT cheaper to leave it on all the time.**

- **TURN OFF unused lights and appliances, especially televisions** - it is NOT more expensive to constantly turn lights on and off.

- **FIT an energy efficient condensing boiler when buying or replacing an old central heating boiler. Saving £100-£130+.**

FACT
Energy use in the home in 1990 contributed 25% of the UK's emissions of CO_2 - the main 'greenhouse gas'

*estimated savings per year all based on average size gas-heated semi-detached house: capital costs not included.
+Cost shown for gas condensing boiler, but oil-fired model also available.

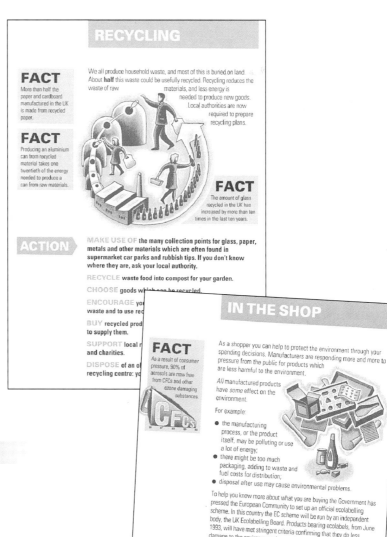

RECYCLING

FACT
More than half the paper and cardboard manufactured in the UK is made from recycled paper.

FACT
Producing an aluminium can from recycled material takes one twentieth of the energy needed to produce a can from raw materials.

We all produce household waste, and most of this is buried on land. About **half** this waste could be usefully recycled. Recycling reduces the waste of raw materials, and less energy is needed to produce new goods. Local authorities are now required to prepare recycling plans.

FACT
The amount of glass recycled in the UK has increased by more than ten times in the last ten years.

ACTION

MAKE USE OF the many collection points for glass, paper, metals and other materials which are often found in supermarket car parks and rubbish tips. If you don't know where they are, ask your local authority.

RECYCLE waste food into compost for your garden.

CHOOSE goods which can be recycled.

ENCOURAGE yo...
waste and to use re...

BUY recycled prod...
to supply them.

SUPPORT local r...
and charities.

DISPOSE of an o...
recycling centre: yo...

IN THE SHOP

FACT
As a result of consumer pressure, 90% of aerosols are now free from CFCs and other ozone damaging substances.

As a shopper you can help to protect the environment through your spending decisions. Manufacturers are responding more and more to pressure from the public for products which are less harmful to the environment.

All manufactured products have *some* effect on the environment.

For example:

- the manufacturing process, or the product itself, may be polluting or use a lot of energy;
- there might be too much packaging, adding to waste and fuel costs for distribution;
- disposal after use may cause environmental problems.

To help you know more about what you are buying the Government has pressed the European Community to set up an official ecolabelling scheme. In this country the EC scheme will be run by an independent body, the UK Ecolabelling Board. Products bearing ecolabels, from June 1993, will have met stringent criteria confirming that they do less damage to the environment than equivalent brands. The criteria are set after examination by independent specialists of all the effects of those products on the environment and full consultation with environment and consumer organisations in the UK and other Member States.

ACTION

When you shop

FIND OUT more about the environmental effect of any product before you buy.

AVOID products with unnecessary or wasteful packaging.

REUSE carrier bags.

CHOOSE water-based or low-solvent paints, glues, varnishes and preservatives.

LOOK OUT for ecolabelled goods.

7

Use information and words from the posters to complete these sentences:

1 Many things you buy can be _____ to the environment.

2 Products with too much _____ use a lot of energy to produce and distribute.

3 Find out if there is anything harmful in a product by writing to the _____.

4 Producing energy also causes _____ _____ to be produced.

5 You can cut energy bills by buying _____ – _____ appliances and by _____ _____ appliances when you are not using them.

6 You can recycle _____ , _____ and _____ by taking them to the _____ _____ in your town or city.

7 _____ uses less energy than producing new articles.

Make the poster you prepared in Activity 8.

8

Choose one of the photographs from Activity 2. In your groups, prepare to make a poster similar to those in Activity 6 telling people about the problem, and giving advice about what to do to prevent it.

Language Summary

Future with *will* and *going to*
Buy recycled products: this **will** encourage manufacturers to supply them.
What is Hong Kong **going to** do about this problem?

see practice page 93

Lesson 2 *The greenest school in Britain*

Language focus: Revision of passives

Skills focus: Reading: finding specific information
Listening for specific information

1

Work in groups of four. When your teacher tells you to start, read the text and answer the questions.

green, green, green...

FAMOUS GREEN THINGS
- Kermit the frog
- Perrier bottles
- Greenfly
- Green Line Coaches
- Phone cards
- Polo mint wrappers
- The Body Shop's biodegradable carrier bags
- The Incredible Hulk

THE WORLD'S GREEN PLACES
- Green Bank, New Jersey, USA
- Green Bay, Bermuda
- Green Bluff, NSW, Australia
- Green Court, Alberta, Canada
- Green Hill, West Indies
- Green Island, Hong Kong
- Green Point, Nigeria
- Green River, New Guinea

GREEN FILMS
- *How Green Was My Valley* with Maureen O'Hara, 1941
- *Green Fire* with Stewart Grainger, 1954
- *Green Grow the Rushes* with Richard Burton 1951
- *Green Hell* with Douglas Fairbanks Jnr, 1940
- *Green Helmet* with Bill Travers 1961
- *Green Card* with Gérard Depardieu 1989

GREEN RECORDS
- Green Fields, The Beverley Sisters 1960
- Green Door, Shakin' Stevens, 1981
- Green Manalishi, Fleetwood Mac, 1970
- Green Green Grass of Home, Tom Jones, 1966
- Green Shirt, Elvis Costello, 1985

EXTRAORDINARILY GREEN
- Biggest greens... a green cabbage weighing 54 kilos was grown in Wiltshire, England, in 1987
- Most expensive greens... an emerald found in Brazil in 1982 was valued at £718,000
- Most fattening greens... the avocado contains 336 calories per kilo
- Tallest green person... Bartley Green, near Birmingham was the birthplace of Britain's tallest woman, Jane Bunford, who died in 1922.

1 Who starred in the film *Green Grow the Rushes* in 1951?

2 Which film starred Gérard Depardieu in 1989?

3 In what year was the song *Green Door* a hit?

4 In which country would you find Green Bluff?

5 Where was an emerald worth £718,000 found in 1982?

6 Where was Britain's tallest woman born?

7 Which green fruit contains 336 calories per kilo?

8 What is the name of a famous green frog?

9 What green thing do you use in Britain to make a phone call?

10 Which shop uses biodegradable green carrier bags?

2

Work in pairs. Think about your school or workplace. What could you do to make it more environmentally-friendly? Add your ideas to this list.

- *Use fewer photocopies*
- *Switch off lights when leaving the classroom or office*

3

You are going to read a text about an environmentally-friendly school in Devon, in the South of England. Read the text quickly and see if any of your ideas from Activity 2 are mentioned.

The Greenest School in Britain

Rubbish is a dirty word at Shute County Primary School – the kids have declared a war on waste...

The kids at Shute County Primary School in Devon are surprisingly quiet when it's time to go home in the afternoon. Instead of the usual shouting and running you can hear them asking each other, 'Are the lights all off?', 'Shall we check the taps in case they are dripping?', 'How many paper towels did we use today?'

But it's not unusual here. The kids have declared a war on waste – every bottle top, bin liner and banana skin has another life.

'We've never made the children do anything,' explains Liz Templar, the school's head teacher. 'They came up with all the ideas themselves. They're doing this because they want to.'

If you take a look around the school you won't see anything thrown away unnecessarily, and no ozone-unfriendly appliances, either. Everything is collected and reused, or sent to be recycled.

Shute school started its green revolution two years ago. They looked carefully at every part of school life – from the teaching to the cleaning. They looked at the way stationery was used – especially photocopying, the way cleaning was carried out, and how food was used – and wasted!

Even parents were scrutinised: how many children came in each car? Did they use unleaded petrol? Could they bring more children in fewer cars?

High on the list was the waste of paper. Next came unfriendly cleaning products. Paper towels were replaced with recycled paper. But the hardest thing for the kids was when they found out how much rubbish was created by the chocolate, crisps and other snacks eaten at lunch time. Of their own accord, the children gave them up. Now they bring apples and home-made snacks.

The school has its own garden where they grow herbs, vegetables and flowers so that they can learn about the environment. They also use this area for their recycling store – large containers to collect aluminium, bottles, paper and fabric.

Even the school's play area is made from recycled things.

Since the children started, the school's heating and lighting bills have fallen dramatically and the number of rubbish bags has gone down from seven a week to two or three.

Everywhere in Shute School there are bright posters asking everyone to take their rubbish home, to save energy and paper and to keep the green flag flying.

4

Read the text more carefully and match these words and phrases with the definitions below. Use the context to help you.

1 dripping (paragraph 1)
2 bin liner (paragraph 2)
3 ozone-unfriendly (paragraph 4)
4 stationery (paragraph 5)
5 scrutinised (paragraph 6)
6 of their own accord (paragraph 7)

a looked at very carefully
b bad for the ozone layer
c deciding themselves
d with drops of water coming out
e large plastic bag for rubbish
f everything you need for writing – eg paper, pens, paper clips, etc.

5

Now listen to four of the pupils from Shute School: Stephanie, Alice, Steven and Paul. They are talking about how this 'green revolution' changed their school life. As you listen, circle the paragraph in the text which each one talks about.

6

The children mention four other ways of helping the environment which don't appear in the text. Listen again and find out what they are.

7

Work with the same partner as for Activity 2. Look again at your list. Can you add anything else to your list after hearing about the Greenest School in Britain?

Homework

Write a letter to the head teacher or principal of your school, or a memo to your boss. Make suggestions in your letter/memo about what you could do to make your school or workplace more environmentally-friendly.

Language Summary

Revision of passives
Everything is **collected** and **reused**.
They looked at the way stationery **was used**.

Purpose clauses
The school has its own garden, **so that** they can learn about the environment.

see practice page 94

Lesson 3 *The techno-solution*

Language focus: Future predictions and possibilities

Skills focus: Reading: note-taking
Speaking: giving an explanation, discussion

1

Work in pairs. Look at these pictures. What do you think is happening, and why?

Compare your ideas with another pair.

2

Read the magazine article quickly to find out what the pictures mean.

THE TECHNO-SOLUTION

1 Americans love technological solutions to problems: if insects are eating the crops, cover the fields with insecticides; if there is a drought, build dams and divert the rivers... So it's not surprising that they are now looking at 'technological solutions' to two of the worst environmental problems in the world today: the greenhouse effect and the destruction of the ozone layer.

2 In a report, the National Research Council is encouraging more study of geo-engineering. They are hoping to find a solution to these problems.

3 The reason why a techno-solution is popular is simple: it promises to solve a problem without asking people to change the things they do every day, even though these are what caused the problem in the beginning. If scientists could find a way to stop sunlight getting through, or reflect it back into space, we could continue burning coal and oil without suffering the problems like droughts, floods, heat waves and killer storms which are caused by the greenhouse effect.

4 So far there has not been much concrete research, but scientists have many ideas. Some are very simple, some are completely outrageous...

5 ■ *Turn Boeing 747s into a special 'environmental air force'. On every flight, passenger planes would release dust or soot into the atmosphere, which would keep the sunlight out.*

■ *Use powerful naval guns to shoot dust into the atmosphere.*

■ *Send billions of metal-coated hydrogen-filled balloons into the stratosphere to reflect sunlight*

■ *Orbit 50,000 mirrors, each 90km^2 to deflect the sun's rays away from the earth.*

These are just some of the ideas.

6 However, some of these ideas would be very expensive and the trouble with techno-solutions is that they can leave a problem worse than before. No one knows what dust might do to the stratosphere, for example. And techno-solutions can be addictive: you use one and you then need another, and then another...

7 Trying to control climates could also cause political problems: who would decide where to have the balloons, or where to release the dust?

8 The NRC, although encouraging more study of geo-engineering, insist that the real answer is to not pollute in the first place. We caused the problems by changing the environment. If we try to change it more, what will happen?

Americans who believe in the magic of technology may find that hard to accept.

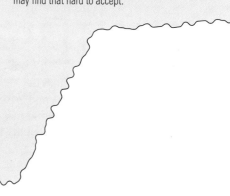

3

Find these words in the text and choose the correct meaning, **a** or **b**.

1 geo-engineering (paragraph 2)
  a the science of trying to change the climate or state of the earth.
  b the science of making engines work with soil.

2 drought (paragraph 3)
  a a person who likes dry weather.
  b a long period of very dry weather.

3 flood (paragraph 3)
  a lots of water covering the land.
  b a good balance of rain and sun.

4 dust (paragraph 5)
  a powder made of very small pieces of waste.
  b very large rocks.

5 metal-coated (paragraph 5)
  a with metal on the outside.
  b with metal on the inside.

Homework

Read this cartoon strip and make sure you understand it. Then write and draw a similar cartoon about one of the environmental issues in Activity 6. Use what you have learnt in Lessons 1 and 2 in this unit to help you.

4

Read the article carefully and make notes under these headings.

Advantages of techno-solutions	Disadvantages of techno-solutions
You don't have to change things you do every day.	

5

Compare your notes with another student, and then discuss these questions.

1 Do you think geo-engineering will solve the environmental problems? Is it a good idea or a bad one?

2 What do you think will happen if scientists carry out any of these projects?

6

Join another pair and work in groups of four. Choose one of the problems below:

destruction of the rainforests   polluted rivers
destruction of wildlife   polluted seas
nuclear waste   rubbish

You have ten minutes to decide on a 'techno-solution' to the problem, and to prepare to describe it to the rest of the class. Your idea can be simple or outrageous! You can make diagrams to show how it would work.

Explain your idea to the rest of the class.

Language Summary

Future predictions and possibilities
  Planes **would** release dust which **would** keep the sunlight out.
  Americans **may** find that hard to accept.
  No one knows what dust **might** do.
  Trying to control climates **could** also cause political problems.

see practice page 95

Language Summary

Question formation

Yes/No questions
Have you seen a film in English?
Do you like working in groups?

Yes/No questions are made from statements. With *be* and *have* (auxiliary verbs) and modal verbs – eg *can, must* – we do this with inversion. With other verbs we use *do/does* with the present simple and *did* with the past simple.

Wh- questions
Which English pop singers do you like?

With question words the word order is

question word		auxiliary		subject		verb
Which	+	*do*	+	*you*	+	*like?*

Subject questions
Who's been studying English the longest in your group?

A subject question asks for the identity of the subject – *who, which, whose, what*. There is no inversion.
Compare:

Who likes listening to songs? – *Reza* does. (*Who* = subject)
What does Reza like? – Reza likes listening to *songs*.
(*What* = object)

1

Does the question word in these questions ask for the subject or the object?

1 Who speaks English in this class? ___S___
2 Which teachers did you like best? ___O___
3 Who taught you last year? _____
4 How many new words do you learn each week? _____
5 Which student makes lists of vocabulary? _____
6 Whose mother has always spoken to him in English?
  _____
7 Who did you find most difficult to understand?
  _____
8 Why do you want to learn English? _____
9 Who will study hardest in your class? _____
10 Which ideas will you use to help you study English?
  _____

2

Look at these advertisements and write questions for each answer.

1 *What type of film is Black Robe* ? It's an adventure film.
2 _____ ? You can watch
  five films.
3 _____ ? The High, Harlow.
4 _____ ? On Sunday at 3.50.
5 _____ ? He gets locked in
  a supermarket.
6 _____ ? Gabriel Byrne and
  Albert Finney.

Mission from God
In the winter of 1634 the Indians made a pact to escort a strange white man on a mission they did not understand. Travelling across 1,500 miles of uncharted French-Canadian wilderness became a test of will for the Jesuit priest the Indians called **BLACK ROBE**.
Lothaire Bluteau stars as the determined priest whose faith and courage are stretched to the limit as he battles to convert the Indians to Christianity.
***Black Robe** is showing at the Odeon only.

ODEON – *The perfect cinema experience*
THE HIGH, HARLOW
24-hour programme information 0279 918437
ACCESS/VISA bookings 0279 948201

SHOWING FROM FRIDAY MAY 5 TO THURS MAY 11

ODEON ONE
Harlow's biggest cinema
SPACE FRIGHT (15)
Weekdays: 1.00, 3.40,
6.10, 8.40
Sunday: 3.40, 6.10, 8.40

ODEON TWO
ALADDIN (U)
Separate Programme
Weekdays: 12.40, 4.10, 8.10
Sunday: 4.10, 8.10

ODEON THREE
TWELVE-TWENTY (18)
Weekdays: 8.10
Sunday: 3.50
BLACK ROBE (15)
All week 6.20
Book now for a late night special

NIGHTMARE ON ELM STREET PARTS IV–VI
NEW TIME: 11.00pm

VIDEOS OUT THIS MONTH

One Wild Night The story of Jim, 21, and already the town failure, who finds himself locked in a supermarket with the local beauty and two psychopathic burglars.

Miller's Crossing A half-comic, half-terrifying gangster film starring Gabriel Byrne as a charismatic wise guy and Albert Finney as the mobster whose mistress he steals.

Vocabulary

3

hear, listen to, look at, watch

Use these verbs in the correct form to complete the sentences.

1 **A:** What does Reza do to learn English?
  B: He often *listens to* songs.
2 In the evening Premi _____ satellite TV.
3 When Osmantan visits London he goes to exhibitions
  to _____ the paintings.
4 **A:** What's Abdullah doing?
  B: He's _____ English radio.
5 When Osmantan visits London he finds it difficult to
  sleep because he can _____ the traffic all night.

Unit 1 Lesson 2

Language Summary 1

Order of adjectives

*It was a **large, square, blue, nylon** suitcase.*

We usually use adjectives in this order:
opinion + size + shape + colour + material + noun

| **beautiful** | **large** | **square** | **blue** | **nylon** | **suitcase** |

1

Put the adjectives into the correct columns.

~~black~~	cotton	fur	green	horrible	large
leather	long	paper	plastic	pretty	round
square	tiny	triangular	ugly	useful	woollen

opinion	size	shape	colour	material
			black	

Can you add any more adjectives to the table?

2

This is a list of things found at a Lost Property Office. Put the adjectives in the correct order.

1 suitcase/square/plastic/black/large
   A large, square, black, plastic suitcase.

2 gloves/leather/brown/small

3 mirror/round/small/black/pretty

4 bag/rectangular/green/small/woollen

3

Look at the picture of Osmantan's jacket and the contents of his pockets. Use the vocabulary in the box to write a description of it.

dark brown	handkerchief	keys
leather	pocket	short	travelcard

Language Summary 2

-ing form and infinitive: verbs which only take one form

*I **managed to remember** the vocabulary for cars.*

Verbs which only take the infinitive often express concern with the future – eg hopes, decisions, offers and plans. Some common verbs in this group are *expect, hope, want, offer, decide, manage.*

*We **practised repeating** new words.*

Verbs which only take the **-ing** form often express concern with the present or immediate past – eg enjoyment, continuity, ending and postponement. Some common verbs in this group are *enjoy, finish, miss, practise, stop, give up.*

4

-ing form or infinitive?

Complete this letter from Osmantan to his English teacher in Turkey, using the correct form of the verb in brackets.

Dear Jennifer,

I've been here for a week and I feel quite happy now. I'm really enjoying (1) ___learning___ (learn) all about Britain. I hope (2) _____ (improve) my English very quickly – they say it's easier in the country itself. Every morning I practise (3) _____ (speak) with the others, and soon I think I'll manage (4) _____ (have) a reasonable conversation! I'm sharing a flat with some English students who have offered (5) _____ (help) me in the evenings if they have time. Nobody smokes here, so I've given up (6) _____ (smoke) too!

I've decided (7) _____ (take) the First Certificate Exam at the end of this term. If I pass, I want (8) _____ (move) up to Manchester and study textile design. My teacher here thinks that when I have finished (9) _____ (study) for the exam, my English will be good enough.

Well, that's all for now. I'm having a great time here but I really miss (10) _____ (eat) Turkish food!

Best wishes,

Osmantan

Language Summary

used to and **would** for past habits and states

*My mother **used to** visit us for three months every year.*
*My parents **would** insist on speaking English at home.*

We use **would** or **used to** to talk about past habits, and repeated actions in the past. We are describing a routine, NOT making a contrast between the past and present.

I'd say a short sentence in English.

We can use the contraction **'d** instead of **would**.

*We **used to** live in England.*

We use **used to**, NOT **would** to talk about states and situations as well as actions, and when we want to point out that the habit has changed now. **Would** can only be used for repeated actions.

*They **didn't use to** see their father very often.*

We use **did** or **didn't + use to** to form questions and negatives.

1

Complete these sentences about Klara using *used to* or *would* and a verb from the box.

| go | hate | have | ~~live~~ | speak | visit |

1 Klara's family _used to_ _live_ in England, but now they live in France.
2 Klara _____ _____ English, but she loves it now and is fluent.
3 When Klara found it difficult to pronounce English words, she _____ _____ tantrums.
4 When Klara and her sister were young, their grandmother _____ _____ them for three months every year.
5 Klara _____ _____ in French when she was with her English grandparents because she didn't like English.
6 Klara and her sister _____ _____ on holiday to England every summer.

2

Underline the text where we could use *would* in place of *used to*.

When I was little I used to live in a small cottage in a village. I <u>used to</u> play with the girl who lived in the house next door. She was French so she used to speak French to her family, but we used to speak English together because I didn't speak French. We used to ride our bicycles everywhere together, but she used to have a better bicycle than me and I was always jealous of her.

When I was seven, my family moved into the town, and I used to only see my friend about once a month. After a couple of years we grew apart: she used to spend more time with other friends, and so did I. Now we live in the same town, but I don't see her much at all, even though I can speak French now!

Vocabulary

3

say, speak, talk, tell

Here are ten sentences. Five are correct and five are incorrect. Can you find the mistakes and correct them?

1 Pam told me she was very angry.
2 'It's very cold today,' Yoshi said.
3 Gabriella said me that she was going on holiday next week.
4 The policeman told to me that he couldn't help.
5 The doctor told me to go home to bed immediately.
6 'I'm not coming back,' David spoke angrily.
7 The teacher told us some good stories.
8 The headmaster spoke to the pupils for two hours.
9 The customer said him that the soup was cold.
10 'Why didn't you say me this before?' Manuel complained.

4

Complete this table of countries, languages and nationalities. Add three more.

Country	Language	Person
England	*English*	*English*
	Spanish	
Japan		
	French	
		Italian
	German	
Greece		
	Turkish	
	Danish	
Hungary		
	Czech	

Language Summary 1

Adjective formation from nouns

*Would you describe yourself as **confident**?*

Many adjectives related to nouns have a distinctive ending –

eg *confidence* → *confid**ent***
   friend → *frien**dly***
   humour → *humor**ous***
   pessimism → *pessimis**tic***
   beauty → *beauti**ful***

1

Complete this table with adjectives made from nouns. You will find all the adjectives in the lesson.

noun	adjective
liveliness	*lively*
confidence	
efficiency	
optimism	
ambition	
sympathy	
competition	
logic	
imagination	

2

Complete these sentences using adjectives from Exercise 1.

1 The secretary was a very ___*efficient*___ typist and never made any mistakes.

2 Joe is so _____ : he always says, 'Everything will be OK'!

3 A teacher has to be very _____ sometimes and try to understand the students' problems.

4 Even if you don't know what you're talking about, try to look _____ in front of the customer.

5 I've never known such an _____ man, he only started with the company six months ago and he's already talking about being a director!

6 We've got a really _____ advertising agent who has some brilliant ideas no one else has thought of!

7 Erik is an excellent salesperson. He's very _____ and always wants to win the big contracts.

8 Mariela is so _____ . She thinks like a computer.

Language Summary 2

-ing form and infinitive with verbs of preference

*I **love to work** closely with others.*
*You **like being** alone.*

We can use either the ***-ing*** form OR the infinitive after verbs of preference – eg *like, love, prefer, hate* to make general statements about habits and choices.

***Would you like to spend** a lot of time in the company of animals?*

We use the infinitive after verbs of preference with ***would*** to refer to specific future possibilities.

3

-ing form or infinitive?

Choose the most appropriate alternative for each sentence below.

1 Jane loves teaching/~~to teach~~, and she would love ~~teaching~~/to teach small children in the future.

2 I'm glad I don't have to work such long hours as doctors do. I'd hate working/to work over eighty hours a week.

3 Ideally I'd like getting/to get a job where I can work outside.

4 I like travelling/to travel but I'd prefer having/to have a job near home.

5 You used to be an accountant, didn't you? Do you prefer working/to work here now? – Yes, but I'd like earning/to earn more money!

6 Don't you like working/to work indoors? – No, I love being/to be outside. I'd like finding/to find a job where I can be outside all the time.

Pronunciation

Each section of a sound which contains a vowel is called a syllable. In some dictionaries dots (·) are used to divide syllables –

eg **ac·coun·tant** has three syllables

   ac·coun·tan·cy has four syllables

4

Complete the table with the words below according to the number of syllables in each.

~~accountant~~ barrister beautician cashier editor florist interpreter jockey lawyer pharmacist photographer plumber poet solicitor surveyor

two syllables	three syllables	four syllables
	accountant	

Language Summary 1

Present perfect simple and present perfect continuous

I've lived here all my life.

We use the present perfect simple to talk about a situation which began in the past and continues up to the present. We also use it when an activity has just finished, or we want to talk about the results.

I've been working with a charity for a long time.

If the situation is unfinished, or temporary, or we want to focus on the duration of the activity, we use the present perfect continuous.

1

Present perfect simple or present perfect continuous?

Read about Richard and Alex, and complete the sentences about them using the correct form of the verbs in brackets.

Richard is a doctor. He works in Charing Cross Hospital, London.

Richard (1) *has been working* (work) in Charing Cross Hospital for fifteen months. He (2) _____ (work) in three different hospitals in the past four years. He (3) _____ (do/already) paediatrics and psychiatry in this hospital, and for the past five months he (4) _____ (work) in surgery. He wants to specialise in care of the elderly, but he (5) _____ (not/do) that yet. He (6) _____ (live) in hospital accommodation since he arrived, but he is hoping to move into his own flat soon.

Alex is a hairdresser. She works in a small salon in Cambridge.

Alex (7) _____ (learn) to cut and style hair since she was sixteen, but she still (8) _____ (not/pass) her hairdressing exams. She (9) _____ (cut) many different people's hair, so she (10) _____ (gain) a lot of experience. One of her best clients is a 60-year-old lady who (11) _____ (come) to the salon every week for sixteen years! Alex really wants to work in a top London salon, but there are very few vacancies. She (12) _____ (apply) for several jobs, but so far she (13) _____ (not/be) lucky.

Language Summary 2

for and *since*

I've been farming **for** three years, **since** dad asked me to help him.

We use **for** when we mention a period of time and **since** when we mention a point in time.

2

Put the time expressions in the table.

1988	a long time	ages	four days
I came to England		I was about sixteen	
	my last birthday		nearly eight months
over twenty years		the beginning of the lesson	
	the last few days	three years	

since	for
1988	*a long time*

Now choose six of the expressions and write sentences about yourself using the present perfect simple or continuous and *since* or *for*.

eg *I've been studying English for three years.*

I've phoned my family every week since I came to England.

_____

_____

_____

_____

_____

_____

_____

_____

_____

_____

Unit 2 Lesson 3

Language Summary

Modal verbs of obligation and advice

*You **have to** have a university degree.*
*You **must** be good at dealing with people.*

We use **must** and **have to** to express obligation or necessity. We normally use *must* when the authority comes from the speaker. We use **have to** when the authority comes from outside the speaker.

*You **needn't** have a specific qualification.*
*You **don't have to** have a teaching qualification.*

We use **needn't** and **don't have to** to show that something is possible but not necessary. *Mustn't* expresses obligation NOT to do something.

*You **should** apply in writing.*

Should is a weaker way to express necessity and give advice – it's a good idea, but not obligatory.

1

A careers counsellor is advising a client what to do at an interview. Complete the sentences using *must, mustn't, should,* or *needn't,* and a verb from the box.

~~arrive~~ ask be phone smoke speak take wear

1 You __must__ __arrive__ on time. You _____
   _____ late.
2 You _____ _____ a suit, but look tidy!
3 You _____ _____ during the interview, even if
   they offer you a cigarette.
4 You _____ always _____ a CV with you, even if
   they don't ask you for one.
5 You _____ _____ clearly and politely; don't be
   too friendly.
6 Don't just answer their questions, you _____
   _____ some yourself.
7 After the interview you _____ _____ them. If
   you've got the job, they will contact you.

2

What qualities do you think you need to do these jobs? Write sentences using *must, have to, should, needn't,* or *don't have to* and expressions from the box.

able to work alone   able to work as part of a team
accurate creative good at dealing with people
good at persuading people   good with your hands
imaginative   have special qualifications
in good health   patient   practical

1 artist *An artist needn't be good with people, but he or*
   she must be creative and imaginative. An artist must be
   good with their hands, and should be able to work alone.

2 hotel receptionist _____
_____
_____

3 nurse _____
_____
_____

4 florist _____
_____
_____

5 salesperson _____
_____
_____

Writing

3

Formal letter of application

Read these two job advertisements from a newspaper called the *Daily Echo* on July 3rd and write a letter of application for one of them. Use the letter form below to help you.

SALES ASSISTANT

Busy central town florist is looking for an enthusiastic sales assistant for our new shop. Must be creative, good with people, with good attention to detail.

Write to: Mrs Anne Walters, Flowerdew, High Street, Royston, Herts.

OVERSEAS SALES MANAGER

Central London. Computer software company seeks Overseas Sales Manager. No experience necessary. Must speak at least two languages. Travel involved.

Write to:
The Personnel Manager, Computron, Tottenham Road, London NW3.

(your phone number)
(your address)
(the date)

(the company's address)

Dear Sir,/Dear Madam,/Dear Mr ...,/Dear Mrs...,

I am writing to apply for the position of ... as advertised in (the newspaper/magazine) *on* (date).

(Introduce yourself, give personal details)

(Say what you are doing at the moment, give details about your responsibilities)

(Write about your work experience and qualifications)

(Say why you think you would be good at the job)

If you require any more information, I would be happy to attend an interview, or you can contact me at the above address.

I look forward to hearing from you.

Yours faithfully, (if you put Dear Sir/Madam)

Yours sincerely, (if you put a name)

(Sign your name, and also write it in CAPITALS underneath)

71

Language Summary

Defining relative clauses

*A coat **that changes colour with the weather**.*
*Massimo Osti is the man **who has brought these fabrics to the shops**.*

A defining relative clause tells us which thing or person the speaker means. We use **who** or **that** for people, **that** or **which** for things.

We can leave out **who, that** or **which** when they are objects in defining relative clauses –
eg *The clothes (**which**) we bought last week.*

1

Join each pair of sentences with *who* for people and *that* for things.

1 I bought a shirt. The shirt changes colour.
   I bought a shirt that changes colour.

2 I'm going to take these shoes back to the shop. The shoes squeak when I walk.

3 This is a very unusual T-shirt. It glows at night.

4 These new fibres are brilliant. Massimo Osti invented them.

5 Golfers need warm clothes. Golfers are now wearing temperature-sensitive sweaters.

6 These tights are impregnated with fragrance. These tights are a new design.

2

Complete these sentences with *who, that*, or *which*. If it is possible to leave out the defining relative clause, write –.

1 Tights _which_ contain vitamin C seem useless to me.
2 Mark was the first person _____ tried the new designs.
3 The colour-changing labels _____ we tried first didn't work.
4 The thermo ski-wear _____ I've worn twice now is absolutely great.
5 The new fabrics _____ are being tried out are helping to keep fashion interesting.
6 These innovative designs _____ are flooding into the shops are wonderful, but expensive.

Vocabulary

3

Label the pictures using the words in the box. Use your dictionary if necessary.

| buckle button buttonhole collar cuff heel |
| hem label lace seam sole strap tongue zip |

Writing

4

Jenny ordered a shirt from a catalogue. When it arrived there were a lot of things wrong with it, so she wrote to the company to complain.

Read the letter and label the parts by putting the correct number in the boxes.

1 The reason for complaining   2 Jenny's address
3 What Jenny wants to happen   4 Why Jenny is writing   5 The catalogue's address   6 The date
7 Ending the letter   8 Starting the letter

> 24 Sheridan Road
> LONDON
> W1C 8LR ☐
>
> Living Catalogue
> 98 High Street
> Bristol BS20 ☐   6th March ☐
>
> Dear Sirs ☐
>
> I am writing to complain about a shirt I ordered from your catalogue. ☐
>
> Firstly it is the wrong colour. I ordered red and you sent me black. Secondly it is the wrong size. I ordered extra large, and you sent me medium. However, my biggest complaint is that the shirt is very badly made. Although I have only tried it on once, one seam has already come undone and part of the hem has come down and frayed. ☐
>
> I am therefore returning it to you. I would appreciate a refund as soon as possible. ☐
>
> I look forward to hearing from you. ☐
>
> Yours faithfully,
> Jenny Evans

Language Summary 1

Open conditionals

*If you **can't** go up, **go** down!*

The basic form of an open conditional sentence is usually:

if CLAUSE		MAIN CLAUSE
if + present simple	+	present simple

We can use modal verbs in either clause –
eg *If I **can** see you, you **can** see me.*
We use this conditional when the situation in the *if*
clause is true or might happen in the future. We can
also use an imperative in the main clause –
eg *If you see Jane, **give** her this book.*

1

**This is Stuart Bexon's advice to a friend who
wants to build an underground house. Complete
his sentences using words from the box.**

ask	can spend	can't get	clean	consult
don't expect	don't need	might consider		

1 If you use my tools, please *clean* them before you give them back.
2 If you haven't got what you need, _____ !
3 _____ to save money if you use cheap materials.
4 If you can design the house yourself, you _____ to use an architect like Quarmby.
5 You _____ more on the rooms if you don't need to worry about the outside.
6 _____ your neighbours if you plan to build anything outside.
7 If you want to save time, you _____ using my plans.
8 If you _____ planning permission, ask Quarmby for advice.

2

**Look at this list of things which Stuart Bexon
wants to do in the future. They are all possibilities.
Write sentences joining the things to do with what
each depends on.**

Things to do	*Depends on*
1 study underground architecture	finding a course nearby
2 build a second home for myself	more people wanting houses like mine
3 invite architects from other countries to see my house	finding a nice location
4 build a second part to my house	time
5 buy the field next to my house	getting approval from the local council
	enough money

1 *Stuart might study underground architecture if he finds a course nearby.*
2 _____
3 _____
4 _____
5 _____
6 _____

Language Summary 2

Participle adjectives

*Quarmby was very **interested**.*
*I found the work very **interesting**.*

Adjectives which end with **-ed** describe the way we feel
about something. Adjectives which end with **-ing** tell us
about the person or thing which made us feel that way.

3

-ed or -ing?

**Complete the sentences below using the correct
form of the adjectives in the box.**

bore	disappoint	interest	satisfy	surprise	tire

1 Stuart Bexon was *disappointed* when he found out that he couldn't build a house on his field.
2 But Mr Quarmby had a very _____ suggestion.
3 When Stuart told his friends about the idea they were very _____ .
4 Mr Bexon found the work very _____ .
5 However, it was also very _____ .
6 'I was never _____ ,' he said. 'No time for that!'

Vocabulary

4

Prepositions of place

**Look at this picture and
complete the text below
with the prepositions
in the box.**

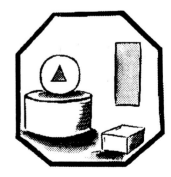

around	inside
next to	on	under

The triangle is _____ the circle which is _____ the
cylinder. _____ the cylinder is the cube which is also
_____ the rectangle. The octagon is _____ all the
other shapes.

Language Summary

Intensifiers

Very large country house.
£450 is much too expensive.
It's small enough to fit in your bag.

We use *too* before adjectives and adverbs and *enough* after adjectives and adverbs.

We use *too much/many* and *enough* before nouns.

This stereo is very expensive. (but I'll buy it.)
This stereo is too expensive. (I won't buy it because I haven't got the money.)

Compare *very* and *too – too* has a negative meaning – *more than necessary* or *more than is good.*

1

Complete these sentences using *very* or *too.*

1 I like this computer, but it's *too* expensive for me. I've only got £500.
2 I'm afraid you're _____ late. I've already sold it.
3 It's _____ modern, with two disk-drives.
4 The computer is _____ good, but the instructions are far _____ complicated: I can't understand them.
5 Are you _____ happy about selling your house?

2

Complete these sentences using *too* or *enough* and an adjective or adverb from the box.

big	complicated	early
expensive	quickly	small

1 This computer is *too* *complicated* for me.
2 This computer is _____ _____ to fit into my pocket!
3 Unfortunately this sofa is _____ _____ for our house. We need one half the size.
4 I've only got £100. The CD-player is just _____ _____ .
5 This laser printer doesn't print _____ _____ : I'd spend all day waiting!
6 I missed the bargains because I didn't get up _____ _____ .

3

Complete these sentences using *too much, too many* or *enough.*

1 We haven't got *enough* time to go and see the computer today.
2 I'd love to buy some new software, but I haven't got _____ money.
3 I can't find _____ information on this computer. We'd better choose a different one.

4 I don't understand this video control, there are _____ buttons on it.
5 You watch _____ television. You should go out more.
6 I'm sure there should be more in this box, there don't seem to be _____ extra parts.
7 You've got _____ computer games, there isn't _____ room for any more.

Vocabulary

4

Add the vocabulary in the box to the word map. Use your dictionary if necessary. Add as many other words as you can.

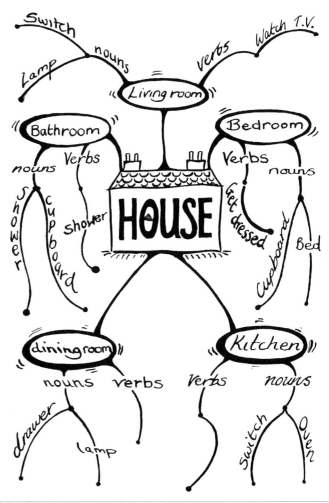

armchair	bake	basin	bath	bedspread	blanket	boil
chest of drawers	chop	coffee table	cooker
cutlery	dine	dream	duvet	eat	entertain
fireplace	freezer	go to the toilet	grill	prepare
relax	shave	sleep	snooze
snore	sofa	rug	toilet	wardrobe

Language Summary

Modals of deduction

*They **could** be soldiers.*

We use **must** to make deductions when we are sure about something.
We use **can't** when we are sure something is impossible.
We use **might** or **may** when we are not sure.
We use **must** or **can't** (or **couldn't**) or **might** + **have** + past participle to make deductions about the past.

1

Answer the questions below using *must* or *can't*.

1 Is Ana playing tennis today? (She's got her racquet with her). *Ana must be playing tennis today because she's got her racquet with her.*

2 Did Peter go swimming this morning? (His swimming costume is dry). *Peter can't have gone swimming this morning because his swimming costume is dry.*

3 Does Jan play basketball? (He's too short). _____

4 Did Miguel like the paintball game? (He's going again next week). _____

5 Has Carolina ever played squash before? (She's got her own squash racquet). _____

6 Are Vasilli and Francesca at the swimming pool? (I've just seen them playing tennis). _____

7 Have Ali and Azim been to the new leisure centre yet? (They don't know where it is). _____

8 Has Emma got her new trainers? (We're going running together this evening). _____

Vocabulary

3

Divide the sports in the box into three groups.

aerobics   American football   basketball   boxing cricket   cycling   football   golf   judo   polo rugby   sailing   squash   swimming table tennis   tennis   volleyball

sports you can practise alone	sports you can play with another player	team sports
aerobics	squash	rugby

4

Answer these questions using the sports from Exercise 3.

In which sport(s) ...

1 do you score goals? *football, polo*

2 do you win by having the lowest score? _____

3 do you need to use music? _____

4 do you need a protective helmet? _____

5 do you play in a small room? _____

6 can a match last for five days? _____

7 must the players wear white clothes? _____

2

Make two deductions each about the sports where you use these pieces of equipment.

1 *It must be a game with a ball, because there's a net. It might be a team game.*

2 _____

3 _____

4 _____

Language Summary 1

Position of adverbs of frequency

Sometimes I do the odd night in a pub.
I never play the fruit machines.
I come here almost every day.

Adverbs of frequency tell us how often something happens. They normally go before a verb, but go AFTER auxiliary verbs and the verb *be*. When there is more than one auxiliary verb, the adverb normally goes after the first auxiliary.

Sometimes, usually, normally, frequently and **occasionally** and adverb phrases – eg **every evening, many times, once a week** – can also go at the beginning or end of a clause.

1

Put the adverbs in the correct place in the sentence. Sometimes more than one answer is possible.

1 I go to the arcade. (sometimes)
  I sometimes go to the arcade.

2 Miguel plays the fruit machines. (never)

3 Alice plays video games. (every day)

4 Catherine has been to this arcade. (many times)

5 Joelle has been to several arcades. (often/in one day)

6 Blake spends more than £10 a week in the arcade. (seldom)

7 Amy is at the same video game. (always/every evening)

8 I must know how much money to limit myself before I start playing. (always)

9 You can find Joe by the fruit machine on the left. (occasionally)

2

Look at these sentences. Are they correct or incorrect? If they are incorrect, correct them.

1 Always the team arrives late for the match.

2 We can sometimes use the outdoor pool.

3 They play video games never.

4 Do you win often your matches?

5 We usually train four evenings a week.

6 He seldom loses a game.

7 They are every day on time.

8 Never they spend more than £5.

9 Occasionally we win easily.

10 I have been many times to this leisure centre.

Language Summary 2

Present simple for habits and routines

*I never **play** the fruit machines.*
*I usually **come** here after school.*

The present simple is used to talk about things we do (or don't do) regularly. We often use adverbs of frequency with this tense to explain how often or when we do something.

3

Ralph has just joined a football school. Read his letter to his parents describing his routine, and fill in the gaps with the verbs in the box.

be	come	compete	do	eat	~~get up~~	give	go
have	help	spend	train	travel	watch		

Dear Mum and Dad,

It's fantastic here! Every day we (1) _get up_ early and (2) _____ straight out for exercises and warm-ups. Then we (3) _____ breakfast – we usually (4) _____ a big breakfast and I (5) _____ always very hungry after the exercises! We usually (6) _____ the morning class doing things like normal schools. Then we (7) _____ all afternoon, either outside on the field or in the gym. Occasionally we (8) _____ to nearby schools for matches.

At the weekend we usually (9) _____ in county schools matches or big competitions. We've won three so far!

In the evenings we sometimes (10) _____ TV or (11) _____ our homework, but once a week a professional sports coach (12) _____ to speak to us. He usually (13) _____ us advice on training and (14) _____ us with our technique.

So, when are you coming to visit me?

See you soon,
Ralph

Language Summary

Defining and non-defining relative clauses

*The pair **who** start must throw the dice and move their counter.*

Defining relative clauses identify nouns. These tell us which person or thing the speaker means. We use **who** or **that** for people and **which** or **that** for things. (See Unit 3 Lesson 1.)

*What is the name of the smallest continent in the world, **which** is the home of the Emperor penguin?*

Non-defining clauses do not identify a person or thing. They give more information about a person or thing already identified.

In non-defining clauses we always use **who** for people and **which** for things (NOT **that**). We cannot leave out **which** or **who**.

In non-defining clauses we put commas (**,**) at the beginning and end of the clause.

1

Are the relative clauses in these sentences defining or non-defining? Write *D* next to the defining relative clauses, and *ND* next to the non-defining ones. Add commas where necessary.

1 The British queen, who lives in Buckingham Palace, is famous all over the world. *ND*
2 The man who invented the steam engine died in 1848. *D*
3 Mickey Mouse who starred in one of the first Disney films is over 50 years old. _____
4 Greece is the country which started the Olympic games. _____
5 The elephant is the animal that has the longest memory. _____
6 The world's largest spider which has a leg span of 27cm lives in South America. _____
7 The cat which lived to the greatest age was owned by someone in the south of England. _____
8 The largest iceberg which was bigger than the size of Belgium was seen in the South Pacific in 1956. _____
9 Big Bill who was the heaviest pig ever recorded weighed over 1,000 kilos. _____
10 The most expensive diamond ever which was sold in 1990 cost $12,760,000. _____

2

Complete the following sentences with *who, which* or *that*. Leave a blank if it is not necessary to use *who, which* or *that*.

1 Christopher Columbus, *who* discovered America, was from Italy.
2 The ship _____ Christopher Columbus travelled in arrived first in the Bahamas.
3 Brazil is the country _____ produces the most coffee.
4 Fleming, the man _____ discovered penicillin, worked at St Mary's Hospital, London.
5 The light bulb, _____ Thomas Eddison invented, is almost the same today as it was then.
6 The Great Fire of London, _____ brought an end to the Plague, was in 1666.
7 The family _____ live next door have just won the largest amount ever in the lottery!

Vocabulary

3

Find these 15 subjects you can study at a university in this puzzle.

biology	chemistry	classics	economics	fine art
history	law	management	mathematics
medicine	modern languages	natural sciences
philosophy	psychology	sociology

M	O	D	E	R	N	L	A	N	G	U	A	G	E	S	N
E	A	H	J	K	L	K	F	N	M	L	P	K	J	O	A
D	M	T	H	V	D	E	N	L	M	V	S	J	D	C	T
I	A	C	H	E	M	I	S	T	R	Y	Y	L	V	I	U
C	N	L	P	E	N	K	G	X	M	C	C	E	R	O	R
I	A	A	H	N	M	B	D	A	G	T	H	C	V	L	A
N	G	S	I	C	V	A	U	Y	T	P	O	P	O	O	L
E	E	S	L	C	D	K	T	F	H	J	L	U	I	G	S
B	M	I	O	G	F	D	B	I	O	L	O	G	Y	Y	C
M	E	C	S	U	T	E	L	N	C	S	G	O	U	Y	I
N	N	S	O	G	S	O	L	E	M	S	Y	K	V	S	E
M	T	T	P	R	S	L	S	A	I	E	N	C	E	S	N
L	H	J	H	O	M	N	B	R	W	K	U	Y	R	E	C
M	H	U	Y	G	C	X	V	T	K	J	H	E	T	V	E
N	I	H	I	S	T	O	R	Y	M	V	Y	R	G	H	S
N	Y	I	E	C	O	N	O	M	I	C	S	H	D	F	S

Language Summary

Time linkers

First she got up and walked around.

We use *first* or *firstly*, *second* or *secondly*, etc. when we want to talk about the order in which things happen.

He looked up as she walked in.

We use *as*, *while* or *when* when things happen at the same time. We normally use while for continuous actions.

After that she whistled, and hummed to herself.

We use *as soon as*, *after (that)* or *before* when things happen one after another.

1

Use each time linker in the box only once to complete these sentences.

after	as	as soon as	before	~~while~~

1 Mrs Crisp was sitting in the waiting room *while* her husband was seeing the dentist.
2 _____ Mrs Crisp went into the dentist's surgery, she asked the other patients if she could go first.
3 _____ Mrs Crisp walked in, the dentist was putting the phone down.
4 The dentist telephoned the Police _____ Mr Crisp floated out of the window.
5 _____ Mrs Crisp saw the dentist's face, she knew something was wrong.

2

Choose the correct time linkers in this paragraph.

When/While I go to the dentist's I am usually quite nervous. Before/While I'm waiting in the waiting room I try to read a magazine, but I can't concentrate very well, and while/as the dentist calls each patient in I get worse and worse. Firstly/Secondly I bite my nails, when/then I usually start drumming my fingers on the chair arm. As soon as/Next the dentist calls my name I feel cold all over, and as/then I'm walking towards his room my legs feel weak. But I'm very lucky, because my dentist is very patient and kind, and he talks to me when/while he's working and makes me feel more relaxed. As soon as/Then I leave, I feel very relieved!

Vocabulary

3

Fear and anger

Match the words from A and B below which are similar in meaning. Use your dictionary to help you.

A	B
1 nervous	a tranquil
2 frightened	b worried
3 petrified	c scared
4 calm	d terrified

Which is the strongest word in each pair?

Now put the words in order from least to most frightened.

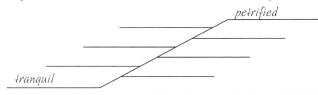

4

Complete these sentences about yourself.

1 I'm frightened of _____ .
2 I'm terrified of _____ .
3 I'm worried about _____ .
4 I'm nervous of _____ .
5 I'm scared of _____ .

5

Use the words in the box to complete the sentences.

~~annoyed~~	anxious	calm	impatient	nervous
	puzzled	relieved	satisfied	

1 I'm so *annoyed* . I want to complain, but I don't know the phone number of the shop.
2 Bill is so _____ . He can never wait for anything.
3 Janik and I are very _____ that all our exams are finished.
4 Jorge's so _____ about going to the dentist that he never makes an appointment until he has really bad toothache!
5 I wish I was as _____ as Gabriella. Nothing annoys her or makes her worried.
6 I'm very _____ . Tim said he would be at home all evening, but there's no reply when I phone.
7 It's been a lot of hard work, but now I've finished, I feel very _____ with the report.
8 Ivan said he would be home at 8pm. It's now midnight and his parents are very _____ .

Unit 5 Lesson 2

Language Summary

Past simple and past continuous

I **was washing** my hands outside when it **happened**.

We can use the past simple and continuous together. The past continuous describes a longer action which was in progress at a past time. The past simple describes a shorter action.

———— past ———————————— ↓ —> present

I **was washing** my hands   when   it **happened**.

We can use **when** or **while** to join the two tenses together. We usually use **when** if a shorter action interrupts a longer one.

1

Past simple or past continuous?

Put the verb in brackets into the correct tense.

The woman (1) _was sitting_ (sit) in the corner of the dentist's waiting room when the receptionist _called_ (call) her name. When she (2) _____ (go into) the dentist's surgery, she (3) _____ (sing) a little song to help her to feel brave.

The dentist (4) _____ (wash) his hands when he suddenly (5) _____ (shout) at Mrs Smith to sit down. Mrs Smith (6) _____ (sit down) at once. She (7) _____ (open) her mouth while the dentist (8) _____ (clean) his instruments.

Suddenly, Mrs Smith (9) _____ (scream), (10) _____ (jump up) and (11) _____ (run out) of the surgery. The dentist (12) _____ (hear) the scream and (13) _____ (say) 'Don't worry, I'm not going to hurt you!' Then he (14) _____ (turn round) to see what the matter was. A huge lion (15) _____ (stand) in the doorway of the surgery. It (16) _____ (watch) him with an angry look in its eye.

2

Complete the first half of the sentences in A with the most suitable ending in B. Then use **when** or **while** and the past simple or past continuous form of the verb in brackets to complete the sentences.

A

Mrs Crisp (drink) a cup of tea

The other patients (wait) patiently

Mr Crisp (see) a nudist camp

The dentist and Mrs Crisp (try) to find Mr Crisp

Mr Crisp (shake) his fist at the pilot

B

Mrs Crisp (talk) to the dentist.

all the patients (go) home.

he (fly) past the passenger jet.

the dentist (phone) the Weather Office.

he (fly) over the South of England.

1   _Mrs Crisp was drinking a cup of tea while the dentist phoned the Weather Office._

2   _____

3   _____

4   _____

5   _____

Pronunciation

Regular past simple verbs

/d/, /t/, /ɪd/

There are three different pronunciations of the **-ed** endings in regular past simple verbs: /d/ – eg **called**, /t/ – eg **liked** and /ɪd/ – eg **wanted**.

3

Write these verbs on the correct line below in the past simple, according to the pronunciation of the past simple ending.

breathe cancel enjoy faint float happen help join jump listen open report scream start

/d/   _breathed,_ _____

/t/   _____

/ɪd/ _____

Vocabulary

4

Here are some of the words associated with teeth and the dentist's. Put them under the correct headings. Use your dictionary to help you.

dental floss drill extract false teeth fill fillings gas gums inject needle polish syringe teeth toothbrush toothpaste

actions	equipment	the mouth
	dental floss	

Language Summary 1

Reported statements

*I **told him** you **were** here.*

When the reporting verb is in the past, the tense in reported speech 'moves back' –

eg present simple → past simple
past simple → past perfect

Modal verbs also change –

eg *can* → *could*
may → *might*
will → *would*

*The dentist **told her that** her husband **would be** unconscious for a while.*

We often use *that* to join a reported speech clause to the rest of the sentence, but after *say* or *tell* we can leave it out.

1

This is what the nurse said to Mr Crisp when he arrived in the waiting room. Change the sentences to report her words.

1 'It's a lovely day.' *She said it was a lovely day.*
2 'I hope you haven't been waiting too long.' _____
3 'You have to have a tooth out.' _____
4 'I'm going to give you some gas.' _____
5 'You can lie back and relax now.' _____
6 'This gas seems a bit strange, so I'll open the window.' _____
7 'I'm just going to get the dentist.' _____

2

Complete the sentences with the correct form of the verbs in the box.

explain	reply	say	~~talk~~	tell

1 I met Mrs Crisp in the street the other day, and we stopped and *talked* for a while.
2 She _____ me that her husband had been to the dentist yesterday.
3 When I asked her how he was she _____ that he was all right now.
4 I thought that Mrs Crisp looked unwell, and she _____ that she had had a worrying day yesterday.
5 She _____ me that Mr Crisp had floated in the sky because he had got the wrong gas at the dentist's.

Language Summary 2

Reported questions

*He **asked me** what the name of the gas **was**.*

In reported questions, the tense also 'moves back' and there is no inversion.

*He **asked me** if you **were** here.*

In reported **Yes/No** questions, we use *if*.

3

Report these questions from the story.

1 'Where is Mr Crisp?' *She wanted to know where Mr. Crisp was.*
2 'Can I go in next?' *Mrs Crisp asked if she* _____
3 'Did he jump out?' *She asked* _____
4 'How could he go up?' *Mrs Crisp asked the dentist* _____
5 'Are you planning a holiday?' *The dentist wondered if* _____

Writing

4

Read this postcard from Mr Crisp and answer the questions.

Dear Mr Huxton,
Having a wonderful time on the South Coast. Nearly collided with a BA plane, but all OK in the end. Seen some wonderful sights from the air, and weather is fantastic! Don't want to come home!
What's the name of that gas you gave me?
Best wishes,
Fred Crisp
P.S. Don't tell my wife where I am!

Mr Huxton
173 Fulham Road
London
W6 8QT

1 Who is he writing to? _____
2 Where is he? _____
3 What is W6 8QT? _____
4 When do we use P.S.? _____

Language Summary

The passive

*Where **is** the baggage **searched**?*
*The books **were examined**.*
*He **won't be prosecuted**.*

We form the passive with ***be*** + the past participle –

Her baggage	*be*	+	past participle
	was		*searched.*

We often use the passive when we do not know, are not interested in, or don't want to say who or what does something (the agent).

If we give the agent, we use ***by*** –
eg *Her baggage was searched **by customs officers**.*

1

Rewrite the following sentences and put the <u>underlined</u> verbs into the passive. They are all in the present tense.

1 At the car park someone <u>gives</u> you a ticket.
  At the car park you are given a ticket.

2 When you arrive at the airport the ground attendant <u>checks in</u> your luggage and <u>reserves</u> a seat for you.

_____

3 Baggage handling staff <u>take</u> the suitcases to the plane and <u>put</u> them <u>into</u> the hold of the aircraft.

_____

4 Security staff <u>check</u> hand luggage and <u>search</u> the passengers.

_____

5 Flight attendants <u>look after</u> the passengers during the flight.

_____

2

Active or passive?

This is Jim Cullon's report about what happened to the man the customs officers caught. Complete it with the correct form of the verb in brackets. Make sure you use the correct tense!

At 10.45 am the luggage from flight BA142 from Amsterdam (1) *was searched* (search) by Customs Officers and dogs. A small bag (2) _____ (find) by one of the dogs, so it (3) _____ (mark) by one of the officers.
We then (4) _____ (go) up to the Customs Hall where passengers (5) _____ (wait) for their bags. We (6) _____ (watch) the passengers to see who the bag belonged to.
The bag (7) _____ (take) by a tall man aged between 26 and 30. I (8) _____ (ask) the man to open it. The bag (9) _____ (search) by one of the other officers and a small bag (10) _____ (find) inside. The man (11) _____ (caution) and (12) _____ (take) into the interrogation room.

Vocabulary

3

Use the words in the box to label the picture of an airport.

arrivals hall	baggage reclaim	check-in desk
customs hall		departure lounge
	flight attendants	information desk
meeting point		
	passengers	passport control
restaurant		
	security check	shopping concourse
sniffer dogs		

Language Summary 1

First conditional

*If prisoners are sent to Chino, they **will have** the chance to become highly-paid commercial divers.*

The basic form of a first conditional sentence is usually:

if	+	present simple	+	will	+	infinitive
If	you	*don't educate*	them, they	'll	just	*return*	to crime.

We use the first conditional when there is a possibility that the situation in the ***if*-clause** will happen in the future. We also use it to explain the consequence of an action.

1

Choose the correct verb form to complete these sentences about baby Steven's possible future.

1 If Steven goes/~~will go~~ to a bad school, he ~~meets~~/will meet children who are naughty.
2 If he spends/will spend a lot of time playing, he doesn't/won't have time for his school work.
3 He gets/will do badly in class if he doesn't/won't spend time working.
4 He starts/will start to do naughty things if he spends/will spend time with naughty children.
5 If he does/will do naughty things when he's young, he commits/will commit crimes when he's older.
6 He gets/will get arrested by the police and they send/will send him to prison if they catch/will catch him.
7 In the future he spends/will spend a long time in prison if he continues/will continue to commit crime.

2

Look at the pictures and write sentences.

1 *If the driver doesn't buy some petrol soon, the car will stop.*

2 _____
_____
_____

3 _____
_____

4 _____
_____
_____

5 _____
_____

Language Summary 2

Revision of *Wh-* questions

Who provides the facilities?
Where will prisoners work?

(See Unit 1 Lesson 1)

3

Complete the questions.

1 Chino Jail is the one jail prisoners want to get into.
   Which jail do prisoners want to get into?
2 Brian Emery was convicted six years ago.
   When was Brian Emery convicted?
3 Other jails teach inmates to sew mailbags.
   What _____
4 Former inmates have started their own companies.
   What _____
5 Inmates learn to dive inside two giant tanks.
   Where _____
6 The US Navy has given equipment to Chino Jail.
   Who _____
7 The scheme has been working for 21 years.
   How long _____
8 Brian Emery has been in prison for six years for robbery.
   Why _____
9 Tony Charles has been in prison three times.
   How many _____
10 Paul Woodley wouldn't want to be a diver because it's dangerous.
   Why _____

Language Summary

Present perfect and past simple

*He's **been** unemployed for over 18 months.*
*A man **has stolen** some toys.*

We use the present perfect when we make a link between past experience and a present situation, and to give news and describe changes.

*In the last three years Ms Madison **has left** her husband nine times.*

We also use it to talk about past experiences where details – eg time, place – are not important.

*He **stole** the toys just before Christmas.*

We use the past simple to give details about a point or period of time in the past.

1

Present perfect or past simple?

Look at an interview between a policeman and Mark Thompson. Choose the correct form of the verb.

Policeman: So, Mr Thompson, you're unemployed.
Thompson: That's right. I worked/have worked for Toy Box for two years, but then they made/have made me redundant.
Policeman: I see. And last week you stole/have stolen some toys from the store.
Thompson: Yes, I'm afraid so. You see, I was/have been unemployed for 18 months and now it's Christmas and I didn't buy/haven't bought any presents for my kids. I know it was/has been stupid…
Policeman: It's a crime, you know.
Thompson: I know. I went/have been to the store twice and I tried/have tried to give the toys back, but the manager didn't accept/hasn't accepted them. I offered/have offered to pay for them the second time, too.
Policeman: Well, we'll see what the manager says…

2

Read the news report and put the verb in brackets into the correct tense.
Good evening. This is the 9 o'clock news.

Several men (1) *have spent* (spent) the night in police cells following the riots in Coventry. A female doctor from Leeds (2) _____ (be) given a five year suspended sentence for administering a fatal overdose to an elderly patient. And in Shropshire a woman (3) _____ (admit) killing her husband after years of abuse. Here are the details.

Riots (4) _____ (break out) in Coventry last night following the election of an extreme right-wing candidate to the city council. Four men (5) _____ (spend) the night in the cells, but police (6) _____ (release) them early this morning.

Dr Mary Jenson, from Leeds, who (7) _____ (give) an overdose to a 75-year-old patient last May, (8) _____ (claim) yesterday in court that it was the patient's wish. The family (9) _____ (say) at the hearing that they (10) _____ (not know) anything about this. The judge (11) _____ (gave) the woman a five-year suspended sentence after the jury (12) _____ (return) a guilty verdict.

And finally, a Shropshire woman (13) _____ (admit) killing her husband. They (14) _____ (have) a violent row which (15) _____ (end) with her shooting him. She is charged with manslaughter.

That's all for now. The next news will be at 10 o'clock.

Vocabulary

3

Complete the word map using the words in the box.

arson	arsonist	assault	*bomb*	burglar
burglary	constable	dagger	fraud	hijacker
hijacking	*kidnapping*	*kidnapper*	life imprisonment	
manslaughter	murderer	offender	probation	
plain clothes detective		rape	*rapist*	revolver
robbery	sergeant	shoplifting	trespass	
suspended sentence		theft	thief	

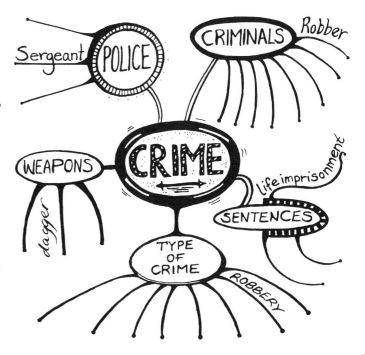

Language Summary 1

Used to + infinitive and *be/get used to + -ing* form

*His father and I **used to** run a pub.*

We use ***used to*** + infinitive to refer to a past habit or state which is now finished or has changed.

*I'm **getting used to treating** him as an adult.*

We use ***be/get used to + -ing*** to mean *be accustomed to*.

*We're **used to** all sorts.*

After ***be/get used to*** we can also use a noun or noun phrase.

1

Put the verbs in brackets into the correct form

1 When James was younger he used to ___*go*___ (go) to school.

2 James' mother and father used to _____ (run) a pub.

3 James got used to _____ (be) teased at school, but he didn't like it.

4 His brother used to _____ (suffer) in the same way.

5 His brother is now used to _____ (be) at school, but James has left.

6 James' parents used to _____ (think) he was strange.

7 Lionel didn't like the idea at first, but he's getting used to _____ (teach) individual classes with James now.

8 Most of James' customers are used to _____ (deal) with him now.

2

Complete these sentences using *used to* + infinitive or *be used to* + *-ing* and the verb in brackets.

1 The first time I met James I was uneasy. I *wasn't used to doing* (do) business with a boy.

2 I _____ _____ (buy) flowers for my restaurant from one of the other florists. Now I use Bow-Kays.

3 James _____ _____ (go) to school, but he didn't like it.

4 'I _____ _____ (study) at home now,' he says, 'and I prefer it.'

5 At school James _____ _____ (do) sport, which he hated.

6 His younger brother says, 'At first I didn't know what to do, but I _____ _____ (help) James with his business now.'

7 James' parents weren't happy about him giving up school, but they _____ _____ (work) with him at home now.

8 James' parents _____ _____ (have) a business themselves, so they can help James with his own.

Language Summary 2

ago and for

*A year **ago** he opened Bow-Kays.*

Ago is an adverb meaning *before now*. It comes after an expression of time. We use ***ago*** with a past tense but NOT the present perfect.

*He's been an antique dealer **for** several years.*

We use ***for*** with the present perfect to talk about things which have continued over a period of time (and may still be true now).

*James went to school **for** about eight years.*

We use ***for*** with the past simple to say how long something continued in the past.

3

Write sentences using *ago* or *for* and the words below. Make sure the verb tense is correct.

1 James' family / move / new house / two years
James' family moved to a new house two years ago.

2 James' family / live / new house / two years
James' family have lived in their new house for two years.

3 James / open / Bow-Kays / one year
_____

4 James / be / in business / one year
_____

5 James / not go / school / over a year
_____

6 James / leave / school / over a year
_____

7 James / stay / at school / almost eight years
_____

8 Lionel / start / teach / James / a year
_____

Vocabulary

4

Interests

Match the hobbies in A with the words associated with them in B. Use a dictionary if necessary.

A	B
knitting	binoculars
flower arranging	cup final
collecting	aria
football	recipe
dancing	vase
cooking	partner
gardening	wool
art	antiques
bird-watching	plants
opera	paints

Language Summary

Comparatives and superlatives

*This is a much **healthier** way of eating.*
*The **greatest** athletes are not just born, but can be made.*

We use **-er** for the comparative form and **-est** for the superlative form of one-syllable adjectives – eg *great* → *greater* → *greatest*.

If a one- or two-syllable adjective ends in **-y**, we change it to an **i** before adding the ending – eg *healthy* → *healthier* → *healthiest*.

If a one-syllable word ends in one vowel + one consonant, we double the final consonant before adding the ending – eg *big* → *bigger* → *biggest*.

If an adjective ends in **e**, we just add **-r** and **-st**.

Most longer adjectives (two syllables or more) take **more** in the comparative form and **most** in the superlative form.

Some adjectives are irregular – eg *good* → **better** → **best**.

We usually use **the** with superlatives.

1

Complete the table with the comparative and superlative forms of the adjectives.

adjective	comparative	superlative
hard tall strict	*harder*	*hardest*
big fat fit thin		
late		
sporty happy heavy healthy unhealthy angry		
relaxing difficult		
good bad		

2

Comparative or superlative?

Complete the sentences with the correct form of the adjectives in brackets.

1 Mikhail's father is _stricter_ (strict) than mine.
2 Todd wants to be _the best_ (good) football player in the USA.
3 Marv thinks that the 'games' Mikhail plays are _____ (healthy) way of keeping him fit, while having a good time.
4 It's much _____ (healthy) for you to eat foods with low fat and sugar content.
5 My brother is _____ (sporty) than me and plays football twice a week.
6 My sister's much _____ (heavy) and _____ (fat) than me, but she's also _____ (fit) because she rides a bicycle every day.
7 Marv wants Mikhail to be _____ (great) athlete in the USA.
8 He doesn't let Mikhail eat sweets because they are _____ (bad) food for your teeth.
9 _____ (difficult) thing for Mikhail will be to avoid eating sweets when he goes to school.
10 Weight-training is a lot _____ (hard) than many sports because it's something you do on your own.
11 I find swimming _____ (relaxing) than most other sports.
12 Todd finds watching TV _____ (relaxing) thing to do in the evening.
13 _____ (late) Mikhail can go to bed is 6pm, because he needs a lot of sleep in order to succeed on the programme.
14 Although it's not as strenuous as some sports, step aerobics is _____ (difficult) because you have to have good co-ordination.
15 In the future, _____ (hard) thing for Todd will be to accept that he can no longer play football.
16 What makes me _____ (angry) is that Marv is a failed athlete, and he's trying to live through his children.

Vocabulary

3

Food and containers

Match the containers with the foods.

a bottle of	chocolates
a tin of	yoghurt
a carton of	wine
a packet of	biscuits
a jar of	tuna
a box of	honey

Language Summary 1

Linking words: conjunctions; contrast, reason and result linkers

*We have **also** started to have rows.*

also, and** and **too link unconnected sentences or phrases, or lists of similar ideas.

*It has been hard **because** we don't have much money.*

because, so, as a result and ***therefore*** link the REASON with the RESULT.

***Although** I love spending time training, I don't have any friends.*
*I feel she hates me **whereas** I do my best to show her I love her.*

although, however, whereas and ***but*** link sentences which CONTRAST each other. Note – *however* usually begins a sentence and is followed by a comma.

1

Complete these paragraphs with linking words from Language Summary 1.

1 Tracy Austin was a star at sixteen. *However* , by 21 she had to give up. She gave up ———— she had a back injury. She became a TV commentator, ———— now she is very happy. She ———— works in advertising.

2 Jennifer Capriati had rows with her parents ———— she never had time to do school work. ———— she loved her parents, she didn't feel free to do what she wanted. She felt they wanted her to succeed at tennis ———— at school, ———— she couldn't do both.

3 Monica Seles moved from the former Yugoslavia to the USA to train, ———— a lot of tennis stars stay in their own country. Her family decided that it was more important for her to move. ————, she was very lonely at first and relied heavily on her family. ———— she soon made friends, she still missed life in her own country.

4 ———— there is no lower age limit, tennis stars are getting younger and younger. Jennifer Capriati was only four when she was given professional coaching, ———— Monica Seles was only thirteen when the family moved to the USA. Tracy Austin, ————, was only sixteen when she won the US Open Championship.

Language Summary 2

should and ***ought to*** for advice

*You **should** try to understand her problems.*

We can use ***should*** and ***ought to*** to give advice or make suggestions.

2

Finish these sentences with your own ideas.
1 Parents should _____
2 Grandparents should _____
3 Children should _____
4 Teachers should _____
5 Politicians should _____
6 Everybody should _____
7 I should _____

Pronunciation

3

Sentence stress

Look at these expressions for showing agreement or disagreement. Put the expressions into three groups.

> Absolutely!   I agree.   I can't accept that.
> I'm not sure.   Impossible!   No, I don't think so.
> Of course not!   Of course!   Perhaps you're right.
> Probably.   There's no doubt.   Well, it depends.
> Yes, definitely!   Yes, I agree.   Yes, I think so too.

agreement	uncertainty	disagreement
Absolutely!		

Some of the expressions have one stress, some two and some three. Practise saying the expressions and put them under the correct heading.

one stress	two stresses	three stresses
Of course!	*Perhaps you're right.*	*No, I don't think so.*

Language Summary

Reporting verbs

Verbs for reporting statements follow several patterns.

*The acupuncturist **told me** that I would feel calmer.*
*She **admitted** that a lot of people felt that.*

Some need an indirect object – eg *advise, inform, promise, tell, warn.*
Some do not need an indirect object – eg *admit, agree, say, complain, explain, point out, deny, promise.*
Some are followed by *for* + another verb in the *-ing* form – eg *apologize* (to someone), *thank* (someone).

*She **advised me** not to go home immediately.*

Verbs for reporting orders, suggestions, and requests are followed by another verb in the infinitive – eg *advise, ask, beg, order, invite, remind, tell, warn.*

1

Change Helen's and the acupuncturist's sentences into reported speech. Use the reporting verbs in brackets.

1 'I drink about four cups of coffee a day.' (admit) *Helen admitted that she drank about four cups of coffee a day.*

2 'I often get headaches.' (complain) *Helen*

3 'I've worked in the office for about three years.' (tell) *Helen*

4 'I've never really liked the job.' (explain) *Helen*

5 'Don't hurt me!' (beg) *Helen*

6 'I'll try to stop biting my nails.' (promise) *Helen*

7 'I haven't stopped biting my nails, I'm afraid.' (admit) *Helen*

8 'I'll continue the treatment for another month.' (say) *Helen*

9 'I'll have to check my diary before making another appointment.' (explain) *Helen*

10 'Eat less carbohydrate and more fresh vegetables.' (advise) *The acupuncturist*

11 'Don't drink more than two cups of coffee a day.' (warn) *The acupuncturist*

2

Change the reported speech into direct speech.

1 She explained that I would have to come regularly.
'You will have to come regularly.'

2 She told me that I should try to stay calm.

3 She advised me to drink less coffee.

4 My friends promised not to laugh.

5 I thanked her for not hurting me.

6 She pointed out that I would sleep better.

7 She explained that I would have to give up smoking.

8 She asked me to try and stop before the next session.

Pronunciation

3

Word stress

Look at these words from the lesson. Mark the main stress in each word.

■
acupressure   acupuncture   acupuncturist   aerobics

alternative   centimetres   extraordinary   insomnia

practice   practitioner

Vocabulary

4

Parts of the body

The following puzzle contains parts of the body. Can you find them?

A	E	D	C	A	L	F	S	N
I	W	A	I	S	T	O	H	A
E	N	K	N	E	E	O	O	I
L	E	G	L	K	J	T	U	L
B	C	B	P	A	L	M	L	T
O	K	N	Q	T	O	E	D	H
W	R	I	S	T	R	L	E	I
P	O	F	I	N	G	E	R	G
T	H	R	O	A	T	S	T	H

Language Summary

Past simple and past perfect

*I **became** a vegetarian six years ago. Before that I **had** always **eaten** meat.*

We use the past perfect to talk about an action or event that took place before another action or point of time in the past.

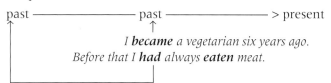

We make the past perfect with **had** + past participle.

1

Past simple or past perfect?

Choose the correct form.

1 The restaurant was closed when they arrived. Their friends had left/~~left~~.
2 Kate had just started cooking dinner when her friends had arrived/arrived.
3 Fortunately her friends brought some wine, because Kate had forgotten/forgot to buy some earlier.
4 Kate had prepared the dessert before they had arrived/arrived.
5 John was late, and when he arrived they had started/started.
6 At the end of the meal all the food had gone/went.
7 After her friends had left, Kate had found/found some garlic bread in the oven that she had forgotten/forgot!

2

Read about Kate's trip to France and put the verbs in brackets into the past perfect or past simple.

When I (1) *went* (go) to France three years ago, I (2) *had already been* (be/already) a vegetarian for two years, so eating meat was out of the question. One night we (3) ———— (go) to visit some friends, Marie and Pierre, and when we (4) ———— (arrive) there Marie (5) ———— (prepare/already) the food. After we (6) ———— (drink) our aperitifs, we (7) ———— (sit) down to eat. I (8) ———— (look) in the kitchen before we (9) ———— (go) to the table, so I (10) ———— (know) that Marie (11) ———— (prepare) a typical French dish made with beef. I (12) ———— (not know) what to say, because I (13) ———— (not/want) to offend them. So, in the end, after we (14) ———— (have) a lovely fresh vegetable soup, I (15) ———— (say) I wasn't feeling well. I (16) ———— (rush) out of the house, and back to the hotel! Next time I'll make sure people know that I don't eat meat!

Vocabulary

3

Expressing your opinion

Choose the correct phrase to complete this conversation.

A: In my opinion/~~It's a fact~~ smoking should be banned in all public places.
B: I don't think you understand./I disagree. People must be allowed to have freedom of choice.
A: Please listen!/But you can't say that. If there are smokers next to you in a restaurant, you are breathing in smoke from their cigarettes.
B: That's not true/I agree – most restaurants have smokers' sections, and besides, if you object, go to another restaurant!
A: I don't think you understand my point./May I say. Why should non-smokers suffer? Smoking is bad for your health.
B: That's not the point,/That may be true, but you can't ban it totally.
A: Why not? In some countries it's illegal to smoke in public places.

4

Food

Put the words in the box under the correct headings in the table.

aubergine beans cauliflower cheese chops cod coffee courgettes cream cucumber eggs flour herb lamb leeks liver nuts raisins rice sausages skimmed milk spaghetti spinach sultanas tea tomatoes tripe veal yoghurt

vegetables	dairy products	meat and fish	other

Unit 8 Lesson 3

Language Summary 1

Adjective prefixes

*Matthew felt very **un**happy.*
*Being **im**patient only causes stress.*

We can form the opposite of some adjectives by adding the prefixes ***un-***, ***im-*** or ***in-*** – eg ***un**fortunate*, ***im**possible*, ***in**tolerant*.

1

Put the adjectives in the box under the correct headings.

> conscious   happy   healthy   kind   lucky
> necessary   patient   ~~possible~~   sensitive   usual

opposites formed with *un-*	opposites formed with *im-*	opposites formed with *in-*
	impossible	

2

Complete the sentences with adjectives from your table above.

1 Some people think Matthew is very *insensitive* because he won't change the order of the waiting list if someone comes to him in great pain.

2 Matthew felt very _____ when his first patient died.

3 Some of his patients are very _____ and want to be well immediately.

4 Matthew's powers are very _____ ; only a very few people are gifted in this way.

5 He says what he does is totally _____ . He doesn't think about it at all.

6 'Most people lead a very _____ lifestyle,' says Matthew. 'I try to teach them ways to help themselves improve it.'

7 'Many people take drugs which are _____ ; they don't need them, all they need is the power of their own mind.'

8 At first Matthew thought he was very _____ because he couldn't lead a normal life, but now he's very grateful and happy to be the way he is.

9 A lot of people think it is _____ to cure yourself without drugs; thousands of people Matthew knows prove that it can work.

Language Summary 2

Articles

*The family always kept **the silver cup** in **a cupboard**.*

We use ***a*** or ***an*** to refer to a singular countable noun – we don't know which one or it doesn't matter which one.

We use ***the*** before a singular or plural noun when both speaker and listener know which specific object is being referred to.

***Scientists** in Canada thought they could help Matthew.*

We don't use an article with plural and uncountable nouns or when talking about things in general.

3

Complete Matthew's words with *a*, *an*, *the* or nothing (–).

'One day (1) ___*a*___ patient came into my therapy room. (2)_____ patient didn't believe I could help him. I said that healing him would need (3)_____ patience and (4)_____ hard work. (5)_____ people often don't have much patience these days, and this can lead to (6)_____ stress. (7)_____ family member can usually help with relaxation techniques. (8)_____ family member which one of my patients chose was his wife. Together, they made (9)_____ effort, and within two weeks there was (10)_____ big difference.'

Vocabulary

4

Match these words with their definitions.

> ~~astrology~~   a healer   a medium
> a poltergeist   a psychic   telepathy

1 A ghost which throws things. *a poltergeist*

2 A person who can talk to spirits. _____

3 A person who can help sick people to get well, usually without medical training. _____

4 The power to understand what another person is thinking. _____

5 The science associated with star signs. _____

6 Able to understand things others cannot, or foresee future events. _____

Unit 9 Lesson 1

Language Summary 1

both, either, neither/nor

We **both** won prizes.

both = *one and the other*. We can use **both** after a subject or object pronoun, and before a plural, countable noun. We use **both of** before *the*, *my*, *those*, etc + a plural noun and before a plural noun – eg *us, them*.

Neither Pauline **nor** Diana liked being a twin.
Ask **either** *of them a question, the answer will be the same.*

either = *one or the other*; *neither* = *not one or the other.*
We use *either* and *neither* before a singular, countable noun. We use *neither of, either of* before plural pronouns.

We use *both...and, either...or, neither...nor*, to link ideas.

1

Complete these sentences using *both, both of, either, either of, neither, neither of.*

1 *Both* Clive and Keith like living in London.
2 *Neither* of them liked being on different ships.
3 In their spare time, they play _____ squash or cricket.
4 Clive and Keith _____ carry copies of the same photo.
5 _____ them know if it is Clive or Keith on the photo, but they say it doesn't matter.
6 When you ask them a question, _____ them will give you the same answer.
7 They _____ tried to work on the same ship in 1952.
8 _____ Pauline nor Diana liked acting.
9 Ask _____ Pauline or Diana, and they _____ reply that they hated being a twin.
10 They _____ hated school because _____ them was treated as an individual.
11 At Christmas, people always gave them _____ the same presents, or very similar ones.

2

Write four sentences about yourself and your best friend using *both, either* **and** *neither.*

eg *We both go to the same language school.*

1 _____
_____
2 _____
_____
3 _____
_____
4 _____
_____

Language Summary 2

so did..., neither/nor did...

I absolutely hated it and **so did** *Diana.*
Keith didn't like that and **neither did** *Clive.*

We use *so* and *neither/nor* to agree with a statement, or to say we are doing the same thing. We use the same tense, or auxiliary, as the statement –
eg *I am reading* → *So am I*
I can swim → *So can I*
I don't like tennis → *Neither do I*
I haven't seen that film → *Nor have I*

3

Agree with these statements.

1 I would hate to be a twin. *So would I* .
2 Keith has never been to Canada. *Neither have I* .
3 I haven't got a twin brother. _____ .
4 We can't tell Clive and Keith apart. _____ .
5 I love the idea of a big family. _____ .
6 Pauline hated school. _____ .
7 If I were a twin, I wouldn't wear the same clothes as my brother or sister. _____ .
8 I had never seen such identical twins before I saw the pictures of Clive and Keith. _____ .
9 I think their story is very interesting. _____ .
10 I would love to meet twins like Clive and Keith.
_____ .

Vocabulary

4

Find words or expressions in the text about Keith and Clive on page 54 which mean:

1 keeping something in good condition (paragraph 1)
_____
2 happening at the same moment (paragraph 1)
_____
3 a place where you can buy and drink alcohol and soft drinks (paragraph 2) _____
4 began our journey (paragraph 2) _____
5 difficult (paragraph 3) _____
6 arranged in the same way as dances for the theatre or ballet (paragraph 4) _____
7 two small organs near the back of the tongue (paragraph 6) _____
8 sewing to hold a cut together (paragraph 7)
_____

Language Summary

Second conditional

*If you **could live** your life again, **would** you prefer to be a man or a woman?*

The basic form of the second conditional is usually *if* + past simple + ***would*** + infinitive.

We can use modals ***could*** or ***might*** instead of ***would*** in the main clause. We can use ***could*** as the past of ***can*** in the ***if*** clause.

We sometimes use ***were*** instead of ***was*** after ***if***.

We use the second conditional to talk about unreal or unlikely present or future situations.

1

Complete these questions with the verbs in the correct tense.

1 If you *lived* (live) in a different part of the world, *would you have* (you/have) the same opportunities as here?
2 If you _____ (not/have) electricity, what _____ (you/do)in the evening?
3 If you _____ (come from) a different country, how _____ (be/your life) different?
4 If you _____ (be) a different sex, what changes _____ (there/be) in your life?
5 If you _____ (can/live) your life again, which two things _____ (you/change)?
6 If you _____ (have) a lot of money to give to charity, which charity _____ (you/choose), and why?
7 If you _____ (be) famous, what _____ (you/do) to maintain your privacy?

2

Write full answers to the questions in Exercise 1.

eg 1 *If I lived in a different part of the world, I wouldn't*
   be able to study English with English speakers.

1 _____
   _____
2 _____
   _____
3 _____
   _____
4 _____
   _____
5 _____
   _____
6 _____
   _____
7 _____
   _____

Vocabulary

3

Ways of speaking

Why do people speak in the following ways? Use your dictionary to help you.

1 shout *People shout so that others can hear them when*
   it is noisy.
2 scream _____
   _____
3 groan _____
   _____
4 whisper _____
   _____
5 cry _____
   _____

4

Adjectives

Put these words from the lesson in the correct column according to the stress pattern.

beautiful ~~brave~~ clever emotional gentle handsome logical powerful quiet rational ruthless strong weak

■	■ ■	■ ■ ■	■ ■ ■ ■
brave			

5

Use adjectives from Exercise 4 to complete these sentences.

1 I'd like to come back as a woman. In the past, women were taught to be *weak* and *gentle*, but now they are much stronger and more assertive.
2 I'd like to come back as a _____ man – then I'd have lots of girlfriends!
3 I'd like to come back as a _____ businessman, someone who always gets what he wants.
4 I'd really like to be a woman again. Men aren't very _____ in this country, and I think it's important to express your feelings.
5 I'd like to be a man, but not now – in the past. I think I'd like to be a _____ soldier fighting for a _____ queen!

Language Summary 1

Conditional sentences without *if*

Tell each other who you **would** *be.*

For imaginary and unreal situations, we can omit the **if** clause if we already know about the condition or if it is clear from the situation.

Conditional sentences with other words

Unless *I put my belt on my hips, I wouldn't look aggressive.*
As long as *I wore men's clothes, people would treat me differently.*

We can use other words instead of **if** in conditional sentences.
unless means *if ... not.*
as long as means *if, but only if.*

1

What would you do in these situations? Write two sentences for each one.

1 You see an accident.
   I would phone the emergency services.
   I would make sure that the people were OK.

2 You see a person shoplifting.
   _____
   _____

3 You lose all your money in a foreign country.
   _____
   _____

4 Your friend asks you to lend him/her a large amount of money.
   _____
   _____

2

Use *if*, *unless* or *as long as* to complete these sentences.

1 *Unless* you wear a tie, you can't come in here.
2 *As long as* you wear smart clothes, you will be treated with respect.
3 _____ Dina wore men's clothes, she would be treated differently.
4 _____ she changed back into women's clothes, she would notice a big difference.
5 _____ she wore very masculine clothes, she wouldn't look like a man.
6 _____ she wore her trousers lower on her hips, she would look masculine.
7 _____ everybody joins in, nobody will feel stupid.
8 _____ you have fun, there is no point in taking part in the *Trading places* day.

Language Summary 2

look, seem, smell, taste, feel, sound

Dina **looked like** *a man.*

These verbs follow this pattern –
verb + adjective – eg It **tastes good**.
verb + *like* + noun – eg It **looks like a vegetable**.
verb + *as if* + clause – eg He **looks as if he's been asleep**.

3

Join a phrase from A with a phrase from B to make sentences.

A	B
That man's really dirty; he looks	like something from the 60s.
What a lovely shirt! It feels	really happy together.
The girl in black looks	as if he's been sleeping on the streets.
I don't know what it is. It looks	delicious.
This pie tastes	too big in these narrow streets.
Rie and Kio seem	like silk.
What an old cassette! It sounds	like someone I know.
Deren seems	like the right man for the job.
Cars and lorries look	like a tool for cutting.

Vocabulary

4

Phrasal verbs – relationships

Complete these sentences with the correct form of the phrasal verbs from the box.

get on with	go out with	grow apart	look after
put up with	settle down	split up	

When Elizabeth met Michael, they (1) *got on with* each other really well. So Elizabeth asked Michael to (2) _____ her. After a year, Michael decided it was time to (3) _____ and get married. However, as time went on they (4) _____ . They didn't seem to have anything in common. Michael always wanted to stay at home and (5) _____ the house whereas Elizabeth wanted to go out and enjoy herself. After a few months, Elizabeth couldn't (6) _____ Michael any more, and they had a big argument. After the argument, Elizabeth and Michael (7) _____ .

Language Summary

Future with *will* and *going to*

*Buy recycled products: this **will** encourage manufacturers to supply them.*

To talk about the future we use ***will*** for:
   predictions – eg *The new airport **will** be finished by 2000.*
   future intentions – eg *I'll start tomorrow.*
   promises – eg *Don't worry, I'll pay you back on Thursday.*
   spontaneous decisions – eg *Do you want another coffee? I'll make you one.*

*What is Hong Kong **going to** do about this problem?*

We use ***going to*** for future plans – eg *Next year we're **going to** visit India.* and predictions from what you can see – eg *Look at the sky – it's **going to** rain.*

1

Choose either *will* or *going to* in these sentences.

1 If we don't start protecting the environment now, the planet will/is going to die.
2 What will you/are you going to do to protect the environment?
3 I will/am going to take my plastic bottles to the recycling point today. Do you want me to take yours?
4 That's a good idea, I will/am going to go with you.
5 I think that by the year 2000, everybody will/is going to have to have more efficient cars.
6 I will/am going to change my car next year – this one doesn't take unleaded petrol.
7 This river has got so much rubbish in it. It looks like it will/is going to die.

2

Complete these dialogues with *will* or *going to* and the verbs in the box.

~~die~~	go	put	start	take	use

1 **A:** There's nothing we can do about the environment: eventually the earth *will   die* .
   B: Don't be so pessimistic! I _____ _____ all my old newspapers in the paper bank – that's a start.
2 **A:** Did you know they've opened a new bottle bank near your house?
   B: No, I didn't. I _____ _____ taking my bottles there.
3 **A:** I don't know what to do with my plastic bottles.
   B: I _____ _____ them to the recycling point for you.
4 **A:** I've decided I _____ _____ my car less.
   B: Good idea. From tomorrow I _____ _____ to work by train, too.

Pronunciation

3

Mark the stress on these words:

■
appliances	biodegradable	carbon dioxide
carrier bags	chemicals	containers
disposable	industrial	ozone layer
pollution	recycled	unleaded petrol

Some words in English have one or more weak sounds in them: the sound /ə/. Mark where this sound is in these words:

/ə/ /ə/
appliances	biodegradable	carbon dioxide
carrier bags	chemicals	containers
disposable	industrial	ozone layer
pollution	recycled	unleaded petrol

Vocabulary

4

Word order

Rewrite these sentences in the correct order.

1 watched Diana a documentary very on environment interesting Jairo and about the TV. *Diana and Jairo watched a very interesting documentary on TV about the environment.*
2 aerosol used didn't damaging know Diana that sprays she were ozone the the layer.
   _____
3 generates Jairo out three tonnes found carbon that one dioxide year person per of.
   _____
4 decided they to four both to each help do things.
   _____
5 glass, metals, paper and now recycle they.
   _____
6 don't which they unnecessary buy have packaging products.
   _____
7 use bulbs turn low-energy off electrical unused they appliances light and.
   _____

Language Summary 1

Revision of passives

*Everything **is collected** and **reused**.*
*They looked at the way stationery **was used**.*

We often use the passive when the action is more important than the agent. (See Unit 6 Lesson 1)

1

Read these passive sentences from the text about the Greenest School in Britain. Rewrite them in the active, saying who is responsible each time.

1 Everything is collected and reused.
   The children collect everything and reuse it.

2 Things are sent to be recycled.

3 They looked at the way stationery was used.

4 Food was wasted.

5 Paper towels were replaced with recycled paper.

6 They found out how much rubbish was created.

2

Rewrite these active sentences in the passive.

1 We all waste too much electricity.
   Too much electricity is wasted.

2 Last year people bought far too many new cars which weren't energy-efficient.

3 Manufacturers use too much packaging for their products.

4 My family uses too many pre-packed foods.

5 Nearly half my school buy too many disposable products.

6 In the past people used less electricity and environmentally-harmful products.

Language Summary 2

Purpose clauses

*The school has its own garden, **so that** they can learn about the environment.*

Purpose clauses tell you WHY something is true. The clause is introduced by **so that** + **can/could** or **in order to** + infinitive.

3

What did the children and teachers at Shute School do to save the environment? Use the pairs of sentences and *so that* + *can/could* or *in order to* + infinitive to make ONE sentence each time.

1 He started using unleaded petrol. He helped save children from lead poisoning.
   He started to use unleaded petrol in order to help
   save children from lead poisoning.
   or *He started to use unleaded petrol so that he could help*
   save children from lead poisoning.

2 The children gave up eating sweets. They threw away less plastic rubbish.

3 The teachers used fewer photocopies. They saved a lot of paper.

4 The parents shared their cars. They used fewer cars.

5 Steven's dad gave up smoking. He cut down on rubbish and pollution.

6 The children decided to use solar calculators. They avoided wasting batteries.

7 The cleaner used environmentally-friendly products. She stopped destroying the ozone layer.

8 The teachers bought board markers which they could refill. They threw away fewer pens.

Language Summary

Future predictions and possibilities

*Planes would release dust which **would** keep the sunlight out.*
*Americans **may** find that hard to accept.*
*No one knows what dust **might** do.*
*Trying to control climates **could** also cause political problems.*

To make predictions about future possibilities we use ***will*** if we are quite sure something will happen, ***may*** or ***might*** if we are not sure, and ***could*** if we think it is possible, but not likely. (See Unit 10 Lesson 1)

1

Rewrite these sentences using the modal verb in brackets.

1 Perhaps the Americans will find a techno-solution. (might)
   The Americans might find a techno-solution.

2 It's possible the hole in the ozone layer will not grow any bigger. (might)
   _____

3 Maybe people are more aware of environmental problems. (could)
   _____

4 Perhaps we still have time to save the planet. (may)
   _____

5 It's a possibility that in the future companies will use more recycled products in packaging. (may)
   _____

6 Perhaps people will buy more energy-efficient cars, and not just the fastest ones available. (might)
   _____

7 It's possible that some people will still be unaware of environmental dangers. (could)
   _____

8 Maybe governments in the future will ban cars. (could)
   _____

9 Perhaps carbon monoxide and methane gas levels will decrease. (might)
   _____

2

Predict what you think *will, may, might* or *could* happen to the people in the pictures. Write two sentences for each picture.

1 *He might get caught.*
  Someone could see him.
  _____

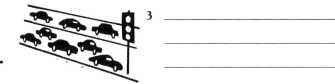

2 _____
  _____
  _____

3 _____
  _____
  _____

4 _____
  _____
  _____

Vocabulary

3

Prepositions of time

Use prepositions from the box to complete this dialogue between a journalist and a scientist. You can use some of the prepositions more than once.

after	at	by	during	for	in	on	until

Journalist: Can you tell me something about how you decided on your techno-solution?

Scientist: Well, the company first had the idea (1) *in* 1990. We wanted to find a solution to the problem of global warming and (2) _____ March the President offered a prize to the team who came up with the best idea. He gave us six months. (3) _____ those six months, my team tried several things. (4) _____ the start we didn't have many ideas, then we worked on one idea (5) _____ six weeks _____ we realised that someone else had built it! (7) _____ that we decided on the idea of the balloons. (8) _____ the end of the fourth month we had a good plan.

Journalist: And when did you learn that you had won the prize?

Scientist: We had been waiting (9) _____ the President's return from the NRC meeting, and finally (10) _____ 7th November we found out we had won.